30

The
Organized
Lawyer

Second Edition

THE
ORGANIZED
LAWYER

SECOND EDITION

Kelly Lynn Anders

CAROLINA ACADEMIC PRESS

Durham, North Carolina

Library of Congress Cataloging-in-Publication Data

Anders, Kelly, author.
The organized lawyer / Kelly Lynn Anders. -- Second edition.
  pages cm
Includes index.
ISBN 978-1-61163-400-6 (alk. paper)
1. Law offices--United States. 2. Office management. I. Title.

KF318.A773 2015
340.068--dc23

                    2015021744

Carolina Academic Press
700 Kent Street
Durham, NC 27701
Telephone (919) 489-7486
Fax (919) 493-5668
www.cap-press.com

To Mom and Gram,
I am honored to follow in your footsteps.

CONTENTS

ACKNOWLEDGMENTS

I am so thankful for the opportunity to publish a second edition of this book, and I am humbled by the depth of support and encouragement from my family and friends. So much has changed in my life since this book was first published six years ago. Through it all, my faith, family, and friends have sustained and strengthened me; for that, I will always be grateful.

First, I thank Lyda Whiteside, my mother and best friend, for being such a wonderful role model, advisor, and confidante. Posthumously, I thank Jeanne Banks, my maternal grandmother, for setting a life-long example of grace, elegance, and kindness that I aspire to emulate each day. I also posthumously thank Charles Banks, my maternal grandfather, for his strength, leadership, and strong organizational skills. They have all provided essential ingredients for the contents of each of my books, including this one.

Professionally, I thank Judge Thomas H. Newton, Charlotte Washington, and everyone else at the Missouri Court of Appeals for such a wonderful clerkship experience. I also thank my friend, Martin Wisneski, for creating and maintaining such an excellent website for my books. Additionally, I am grateful to the Jackson County Law Library Board for the opportunity to serve as the library's Executive Director, and to my colleague and friend, Dale Magariel, for her warmth and professionalism.

Finally, I am grateful to the libraries and readers around the world who have purchased my books, and to the many reviewers who have provided positive comments. I also thank everyone at Carolina Academic Press for always being such a pleasure to work with.

A mind once stretched by a new idea never regains its original dimension.

Oliver Wendell Holmes, Jr.

Introduction

Picture a workspace with stacks of papers, mounds of magazines, wayward files, and only the hint of a desktop. Every drawer is a "junk" drawer, and there's no such thing as a clear space. Sometimes, it is embarrassing when visitors stop by, but who has time to clean? Being organized isn't a priority; time is better spent on "more important" tasks. It would be wonderful to have a place for things and to feel the sense of pride, peace, and control that comes from a serene space, but who knows where to begin?

Sound familiar?

There's more than one way to be organized, but you wouldn't know it from most books and television shows. There's so much more to creating and maintaining an organized space than purchasing a bunch of plastic bins and attractive containers from the local office supply store. Add stress and time constraints and multiple types of items to control and it's a recipe for failure—or a belief that organization is impossible.

It all starts in law school—or possibly before. We all remember first year. So much information to process, and a new language to learn. Typically used words like "consideration" took on new meanings and we were introduced to countless new ones. Enormous amounts of information is located in books, papers, notebooks, laptops, computers, and bags, and even in luggage for those who opt to wheel their gear around from place to place. In addition to the luggage, some also use the trunks of their cars and a locker at school for additional storage. The average textbooks in law school must be sold by the pound because they are as heavy as they are expensive.

So, information overload begins the day you set foot through the door of your law school—and feeling lost and helpless in managing that information is just as immediate. I know that's how I felt. And that was back in the days when it was considered cutting-edge to own a computer with 32 megs of RAM, there was no such thing as a law school web page, the Internet was in its infancy, and cell phones looked more like bricks than communication devices. Now, we're tuned in, online, hooked up, and essentially accessible 24 hours a day—and challenges with information overload only promise to increase.[1] However, unlike other professions, lawyers cannot simply choose one method of communication or information storage over all others because the law is practiced in all forms due to tradition and necessity. As a result, records must be kept in print, electronically, and in various forms of the two. And lest us not forget billable hours—although many would like to.[2]

During this same period of time, the amount of space we have to work with has decreased.[3] In many workplaces, offices are smaller, cubicles are the norm, and, like other professions, the legal profession lacks the stability it used to enjoy.[4] So, not only is there more information to manage, but there's less space in which to do it, and, because of job movement, that information is passed on in various forms of disarray from one person to the next. It then becomes your responsibility to get your inherited information in order so that you can do a competent job—all the while

---

1. *See, e.g.*, Steve Lohr, *Is Information Overload a $650 Billion Drag on the Economy?* THE NEW YORK TIMES, December 20, 2007; David Lavenda, *Too Many Apps: The New World of Information Overload*, CMS WIRE, February 23, 2015.

2. *See* ABA COMMISSION ON BILLABLE HOURS REPORT 2001–2002. *See also* Scott Turow, *The Billable Hour Must Die*, ABA JOURNAL, August 2007; Robert E. Hirshon, *The Billable Hour is Dead. Long Live ... ?* GP SOLO, January/February 2013.

3. *See* Jill Schachner Chanen, *The New Office: Today's Interior Design Trends Promote Efficiency, Collegiality—Even Conservation*, ABA JOURNAL, July 2005; Erin Coe, *Law Firms Cut Office Space to Gain Efficiency*, LAW360, November 29, 2011; Brandon Gee, *No Room for Egos in Law Office of the Future*, DETROIT LEGAL NEWS, September 26, 2014.

4. *See, e.g.*, Steven J. Harper, THE LAWYER BUBBLE: A PROFESSION IN CRISIS (Basic Books, 2013).

maintaining your other files, e-mails, snail (or postal) mail, books, cases, articles, client communications, notes, meeting materials, billable hours, trust accounts, employee records, personal accounts, business cards, pens, letterhead, office supplies, cell phone, post-it notes, and other "essential incidentals." How does one prioritize all of these competing interests and maintain a workspace that inspires confidence from clients who depend on us and colleagues we are either trying to impress or by whom we at least want to appear capable, reliable, and on top of our game?

Sadly, many of us are dropping the ball. On a regular basis, attorneys are sanctioned for many misdeeds that can be traced back to disorganization. Often, the sanctions are for actions that are inexcusable, but not malicious. Rather they are examples of how bad things can get when one is disorganized. Examples include commingling of funds, failure to produce records to opposing counsel, failure to file in a timely manner, being inaccessible to clients, and seeming ill prepared to represent clients during hearings. Just the thought of all of the responsibilities we need to handle can be overwhelming. How does one do so and remain organized?

Many attorneys rely on their assistants or colleagues. But nothing replaces the confidence of knowing where things are and having a comfortable command of one's surroundings. Not only is it essential for you as the attorney, it also helps colleagues, assistants, and, most importantly, clients. Even though they come to you under stress from their problems, they do notice the order (or disorder) of your office—and they make judgments about your competency from what they see.[5]

---

5. *See, e.g.*, Mark Bassingthwaighte, *Keep Malpractice and Disciplinary Problems at Bay: To Reduce the Risk of Legal Malpractice Lawsuits and Ethics Complaints, Take a Hard Look at Your Firm's Weaknesses and Vulnerabilities, Starting with the Way You Keep Track of Substantive Issues and How You Take Care of Your Clients*, TRIAL MAGAZINE, January 1, 2008 (stating, "Some lawyers view a messy desk and cluttered office as a badge of honor and believe that stacks of files on a lawyer's desk imply that he or she is in demand.... [A] messy office can also create a negative impression. If a client's case takes

No one expects to see a space that is entirely clutter-free, but most people feel more comfortable in an office that offers a clean chair, small space to lean or set down personal items, and surroundings that demonstrate control over one's workload. When a client comes to you for help, he or she wants to feel like you can handle it. How can they be expected to trust you with life-impacting decisions when you don't appear to have control of your own affairs? That may sound harsh, but perceptions matter—especially in the legal profession.

That's where this book comes in. *The Organized Lawyer* is designed to address the needs of all types of lawyers and at every point in their careers. There will be useful tips for first-year law students to seasoned senior partners. Whether you're in a cubicle, corner office, or working out of your home, this book will help you develop and maintain a more organized space.

Much has changed in the legal field since the first edition of this book was published in 2009. Back then, law firm layoffs were merely a faint possibility on the horizon instead of a common— and an unfortunate—reality. Law schools were not as focused on the development of "practice-ready" lawyers, while practical skills are now beginning to routinely receive the respect that they deserve in the legal academy. Finally, firm consolidations were not as prevalent.

Despite these changes—and, perhaps, also because of them— the importance of developing strong organizational skills continues to be of the utmost importance for lawyers. This is true for those in all areas of practice, and at all levels. But one misconception warrants clarification before proceeding further: *Organization is not about cleaning.* This is what keeps many lawyers from developing organizational skills that will last a lifetime. Instead, organization is a process that takes thought, time, and honesty on the

---

a turn for the worse, the client is likely to conclude that the bad result was due to the attorney's failure to devote adequate time to the representation— and the attorney's office can confirm that notion."). *See also* Alina Tugend, *Too Busy to Notice You're Too Busy*, THE NEW YORK TIMES, March 31, 2007; Alicia J. Gipe, *Clearing Stress Starts With Your Desk*, THE DAILY RECORD, February 24, 2015.

front end. If performed effectively, this planning process will be simple to maintain on a daily basis, with minimal needs for drastic maintenance.

It first begins with an honest assessment of where you are, what you're willing to do to alter, improve, and maintain your workspace(s), and an acknowledgment of the importance of the *appearance* of organization. This is yet another misconception. Organization does not only refer to being organized; it requires the appearance of organization to net the most benefits. Many people claim to know where things are located, but their workspaces lack the appearance of order that would elicit confidence from clients and colleagues as to the degree of their professionalism and command of their workspace(s) and belongings.

Throughout the book, I will neither judge nor nudge—my only aim is to speak candidly with you about your relationship with the items around you. In the process, we will explore (and hopefully resolve) three issues: (1) What does it mean to be organized? (2) Why does it matter? (3) How are lawyers different?

In addition to focusing on the needs of lawyers and lawyers-to-be, what also sets this book apart from other organizational guides is its approach. Many books offer valuable tips and tools, but they fail to address how different people have different ways of looking at their things. I believe we all have a particular organizational type that impacts how we view our things, live with them, and keep them organized—or disorganized. What works for some does not work for others. For this reason, the next chapter focuses on the four primary organizational types and includes a brief quiz to help you determine your particular type. It will also help you to determine how you are most comfortable with items in your work environment, how you treat these items when you are under stress, and what it will take to keep you organized. I personally do not believe one method fits all. Some people need open storage, while others need closed storage. This is just one example of how our particular organizational type influences our surroundings and can be used to our benefit in developing and maintaining an organized workspace.

Once you have completed the questionnaire in Chapter 1 and know your type, you may then skip around to review chapters in the order that best suits your needs. You may find that you see yourself in more than one type, but please follow the guidelines for your primary type when reviewing the rules in each chapter. As you will see, the topics are broad—and intentionally so. I have tried to address every direct and indirect issue associated with what it may take for you to become and remain an organized lawyer.

In Chapter 2, we will review various office layouts, as well as the best ones for various organizational types. Chapter 3 covers desk arrangements, including detailed descriptions of the many options for the placement of items, recommended contents for the desktop and drawers, and the best ones for your type. We will also address ideas for steps to take when you cannot rearrange your space to best suit your type. The next section of the book discusses the management of information, including paper and electronic files, financial recordkeeping, billable hours, and the use of print and electronic organizers.

Chapter 7 offers tips for home offices, and Chapter 8 discusses the use of alternative work areas so that you can keep organized when you're away from an office setting. Chapter 9 covers your home and office libraries, including suggestions for contents and tips for keeping them organized.

We will discuss marketing and client development in Chapter 10. Whether entertaining clients and colleagues in the office, at home, or in a separate venue, there are crucial considerations to ensure things go smoothly. Additionally, this chapter will include tips on best practices for the professional use of social media.

An attorney's professional wardrobe will be addressed in Chapter 11. Although there are a variety of "dress for success" guides available, there are none that focus on the needs of attorneys. This chapter will provide an overview of a few of the most useful guides, as well as checklists for men and women for recommended wardrobe items. (And, yes, we will discuss ways to keep them organized.) The last chapter, "Just the Beginning," offers methods to stay organized.

Regardless of whether you do a complete overhaul of all of your workspaces or if you simply reorganize one desk drawer, my hope is that you will finish this book with a better understanding of what it will take for you to become and remain an organized lawyer.

Are you ready to begin?

Life isn't about finding yourself. Life is about creating yourself.

George Bernard Shaw

CHAPTER 1

YOUR ORGANIZATIONAL TYPE

Before you can become and remain organized, it is crucial to know how you most comfortably live among your things. Some of you might be thinking, "That's easy. I am most comfortable among clutter!" But it's not that simple. What kinds of items are present? Is the collection a haphazard compilation, or is it limited to items that fall into distinct categories? How does your space change when you are busy? What's on your walls? What's on your desk? How do you use binders, notepads, and post-it notes? Perhaps most importantly, what do you want to look at each day, and how does this image compare to what you currently see?

As you can see, great organization takes a lot of thought. You need to understand yourself and think through how you work on a daily basis before starting to physically alter your surroundings.

This chapter will focus on helping you to determine your personal organizational type. Yes, believe it or not, there are distinct tendencies and patterns that can be found among what you thought was just a simple mess. Cleaning up a space is great, and it gives us a wonderful feeling of accomplishment and order. However, living and working in that space on a daily basis can quickly turn that same clean, orderly space right back into the compilation of clutter that it once was if we make the same *decisions* (notice how I did not say "the same *mistakes*") each day.

Although you may be looking at a complete mess right now, that does not mean that you are incapable of maintaining an orderly space. What it does mean is that you are not aware of how you view and use your things, and the items used for storage and organization are not best suited to your personal organizational

13

type. That's not to say that you are completely blameless. You will, after all, need to do your part to maintain your space once it is organized. But that task is so much easier when you use the tools that come most naturally to you.

That's where your personal organizational type comes in. It concerns how you store your things when you are feeling the most organized, how you live among the rubble, what you tend to do with your belongings when under stress, and how others might be feeling when they are in your workspace.

Of course, these types could also be applied to non-lawyers, but there are many resources that focus on the organizational needs of the general public, with few that focus on the legal profession. As a group, lawyers tend to handle challenges privately.[1] I can't help but wonder if the Socratic Method is partially to blame because most lawyers vividly remember the discomfort and even shame associated with not knowing the answers when asked during law school. I suspect some might be equally uncomfortable with openly disclosing a lack of knowledge about what to do about a disorderly office.

By responding to the following series of questions, you're taking a very important step to becoming more organized. Most of the advice in this book is based on your particular organizational type. The vast majority of people will have a general type, with tendencies that lean toward another type when they are faced with the greatest number of projects. But the primary type is what you should focus on to have a better understanding of how you view the items around you. After the questionnaire, types will be discussed in greater detail, including their unique attributes and challenges.

---

1. For an extensive analysis of various lawyer tendencies and motivations, see Susan Swaim Daicoff, LAWYER, KNOW THYSELF: A PSYCHOLOGICAL ANALYSIS OF PERSONALITY STRENGTHS AND WEAKNESSES (American Psychological Association, January 2004).

Questionnaire: Determine Your Organizational Type

To help you determine your personal organizational type, I have developed the following series of questions. Much like instructions we remember from the LSAT, please choose the *best* answer. In contrast to that dreaded test, no response is incorrect. If more than one seems like the best answer, choose the one that is most like you under the greatest amount of stress. Most importantly, be honest. Don't answer how you'd like to be, but rather how you really are. When you're finished, tally the total number of A's, B's, C's, and D's to determine your type. Remember—there's nothing wrong with you or your things. We're just trying to pinpoint ways to make your space more of a visual statement of the capable and conscientious attorney that you are.

1. The last time I cleaned anything on my desk was:
   A. Today
   B. Last week
   C. At least a month ago
   D. Cleaned?

2. The items on the walls in my workspace include:
   A. Artwork that I have selected, awards, my framed degrees and certificates, and a bulletin board
   B. A calendar and artwork that my employer owns
   C. Posters and other materials that focus on a few subjects that are of the greatest interest to me
   D. Eclectic artwork, cartoons, posters, drawings by my children, and a bulletin board with so many items on it that I cannot see the background

3. The colors of my files:
   A. Vary because I prefer to color-coding everything so that I can see what I am working with
   B. Don't really matter to me because I tend not to put anything away anyway

   C. Are the usual colors of manila and green, I guess, but I am much more concerned with the contents and topics
   D. Vary because I use colored files for different reasons. For example, one color may just appeal to me because it reminds me of a favorite sweater or my spouse's eyes. Nothing has to match.

4. What is kept on the floor of your workspace?
   A. Piles that are separated based on topic
   B. Stacks of items that I don't work with on a regular basis
   C. Stacks of books and magazines
   D. You name it

5. When people visit my office, my guest chair is:
   A. Usually free of clutter, unless I happen to have items there temporarily
   B. Available, primarily because I have several of them
   C. Stacked with books and papers that I put there a few days ago
   D. Usually unavailable, and people tend to have to wait for me to put the contents on the floor so that they can be seated

6. I hang my coat:
   A. Neatly in my office
   B. On my chair
   C. On my guest chair
   D. Wherever there's an open space

7. When I am away from the office, people can find things:
   A. In stacks and files
   B. In stacks and spread across my desk
   C. In stacks, all over my desk, and on the floor
   D. In haphazard places because I tend not to designate places for things

8. My home office is:
   A. Full of stacks of papers that I need to weed through
   B. A jumbled mess of papers spread out on the top of my desk or table

    C. Full of books and magazines on my areas of expertise
       that I can't seem to part with
    D. Full of mementos, family photos, and knick-knacks, plus
       papers and reading materials

9. My books are taking over my workspace because:
    A. They are in tall stacks
    B. They are spread around the room
    C. There are so many that fascinate me
    D. I can't seem to throw any of them away

10. When I write notes by hand, I use:
    A A notepad that I keep intact
    B. A notepad or post-it notes that I tear off and place with
       other items
    C. A notepad that I received from a conference
    D. A notepad or post-it notes that I received as a gift

To determine your type, add up the numbers of A's, B's, C's, and D's.

Mostly A's: Stacker

As the name implies, Stackers like to place items in ... stacks. These stacks and piles can be vertical or horizontal, and they often like to arrange items by topic or project. The busier they are, the more stacks they'll have. However, these stacks may not always be sitting out in the open. Empty space on a Stacker's desk does not translate into a clean slate with nothing to do. On the contrary, this type has a knack for concealing stacks, or keeping projects so neatly (or seemingly neatly) stacked in piles that it is very difficult to know just how much is on their plates or how many projects they may be juggling at a given time.

Stackers are both visual and tactile because they like the appearance of order and have a need to actually see it, and they must touch their papers and files to have a physical handle on where their things are located.

When under stress, Stackers may occasionally compile stacks that are haphazardly arranged into neat formations that must be looked through later, but the more of these mysterious compilations that exist, the more stressed Stackers become. This type feels a need to know what is in each pile, and derives an intense satisfaction with feeling a sense of control over the belongings in his or her workspace.

Mostly B's: Spreader

Like Stackers, Spreaders are very visual—so much so, in fact, that they must literally see everything they are working on while they are immersed in a task. It's easy to tell what has their primary attention at a given moment because it will be spread across their desk. This does not mean that it is easy to know what, exactly, is on their desks, and therein lies the problem.

As projects increase, so do the spreads, until even the Spreader has trouble locating documents on his or her desk. Eventually, all of the papers look alike, and the Spreader feels stressed and frustrated as he or she pushes papers aside to find the needle in the haystack. Unfortunately, this often occurs at the wrong time—in front of clients or colleagues—making the spreader appear rushed and harried when in fact he or she is simply frustrated because of an inability to find a relevant document the moment it is needed.

At first glance, Spreaders may be mistaken for Stackers because they do have neat piles in their offices, and they often have very attractive bookshelves that appear to be in pristine, or at least neat, condition. But these are simply materials that are not used on a daily basis. Anything in current use is opened or spread out. When they tidy up their space, Spreaders will tend to create stacks, but anything commanding immediate attention will not stay that way.

Mostly C's: Free Spirit

Free Spirits are idea lovers who are immersed in a few areas of specialization. They are so focused on their key one or two specialties that they either don't notice the rubble around them, or they care less about the mess than the subject at hand. Free Spirits have an intellectual tie to their things. Each item is kept nearby because it is considered important for a current project, it was previously important and not discarded, or it is simply considered interesting enough to keep around.

Items in a Free Spirit's office can be kept in haphazard stacks, in bookshelves, on walls, and on the floor. Typically, the newest additions are on the top of each compilation. Free Spirits can have items in various forms on different days. They seldom have a pattern that makes sense to anyone else but themselves.

This type may also become overwhelmed by wayward post-it notes, which are often placed on the computer monitor, in books, on the desktop, and on various documents. These are thoughts and notes that came to mind while working that the Free Spirit wanted to jot down and remember, but there are so many notes, that he or she often misplaces them or forgets which ones have the notes that are needed at a given time. The well-meaning Free Spirit has every intention—whether realistic or not—of getting to all of these intriguing newspapers, magazines, books, and other items stacked on the floor and atop every surface of furniture—eventually.

Mostly D's: Packrat

In contrast to other organizational types, Packrats have an emotional tie to their things. Many, if not most, of the items they display or use on a regular basis have an emotional tie or meaning. While it is common for most of us to keep special photos or small mementos in our workspaces, Packrats take this concept a step further. They may have special art, use a pen or a notepad that was a gift from a loved one, or they may have memorabilia from a favorite film or television show nearby for personal reasons. As an example, I have known of people who display collections of *Star Trek* or Disney memorabilia in their offices. This can add a touch of whimsy or charm when used sparingly, but it can be distracting to visitors when such displays get out of control.

Since many items surrounding a Packrat in his or her workspace hold personal meaning and importance, anyone coming into their work environment can be taken by surprise by how seemingly random and haphazard this grouping appears, but it makes perfect sense to the Packrat. Not ones who like empty spaces, Packrats tend to pile things around themselves, as if creating some sort of protective fortress or cocoon, and seldom do they take the time to stack things neatly. While others may see this as a hopeless mess, many Packrats feel a small sense of pride with not being perfectly neat. For this type, neatness can feel cold and not "lived in" or personalized. The greatest challenge Packrats face is not having a system that is easy for others to follow or understand.

Starting the Organization Process

Now that you know your organizational type, we're going to focus on how to start working with it. As I have mentioned, there is nothing wrong with any type. The only mistakes you can make are either trying to force yourself to be something that you're not or using organizational tools that are not naturally suited to your style. Both of these mistakes are recipes for failure—and a misconception that you are incapable of creating and maintaining an organized workspace.

Before you start ripping your office apart, take a moment to really think about your personal type. Remember, *organization takes thought and time.* So, the first thing to do is to allow this information to sink in. Read about the other types to see how they compare and contrast with yours. Visit your colleagues' workspaces and observe their things. If you're still in law school, visit and observe your professors' offices—but don't try to correct them!

Ideally, you will spend about a week processing this information. Although it's tempting to make immediate changes, the most important thing you can do at this point is to live among your things in their current state to absorb this information and allow yourself to see your things and your surroundings for how they really are. Ask a few friends and relatives to give you honest feedback about how they feel when they are in your workspace. I would not recommend asking clients because they are depending on you to professionally represent them, and any organization projects are best handled outside of the attorney-client relationship. Instead, allow your new workspace to eventually speak for itself.

Try not to be too hard on yourself as you live among your things in their "before" or current state. You are to be commended for taking this important step, and from now on you will always view yourself and your surroundings differently—and in a much more positive light.

Be especially mindful of small, daily activities. What do you need to push aside or hunt for when the phone rings? How do you leave your space at the end of the day? What is the first thing you do when you arrive in the morning? Do you recycle? How heavily do you rely on electronic devices, including the computer? What do you take with you to meetings? If someone needed to find something in your office, how easily could it be located? Do you typically re-file documents in your workspace, or is this an unrealistic expectation on a daily basis? How much time is spent writing, reading, and responding to e-mail? Do you type your own documents, or delegate that and other general tasks to an assistant?

If you're still in law school, are you an assistant to someone else? What is his or her organizational type, and what steps could you take to work together more smoothly? Of course, since your supervisor may not have taken the Organization Questionnaire, this requires some degree of speculation, which may not be completely fair or accurate. If you have a comfortable rapport, you might consider asking him or her to take it so that you two can work together more efficiently. Some might decline the offer, but others will be open to the idea. As attorneys, every minute counts—literally—so timesavers are crucial, and your initiative may be rewarded in surprising ways.

The First Step: Clearing the Desk

After this initial period of living among your things in their current state, continue to keep everything as-is, except the surface of your desk. Get a large box, basket, or bin and take everything off of the top of your desk except your telephone and computer. Use plastic sandwich bags to hold small items so that they do not rattle around in the box, and so that you can retrieve them when you need them. Once your desk has been cleared off, clean the surface with whatever cleaner it was designed to handle—Windex, furniture polish, etc. Keep the box at your feet so that you can retrieve items when needed, but for now, keep the surface of your desk completely empty. Clearing and cleaning your desk could take 10 minutes or half a day, depending on what is there.

Why am I asking you to do this? First, because I want you to experience how it feels to start with a clean and fresh space, even in a small way. I also want you to get a feel for what it will be like to organize the rest of your space. It's going to take work, but it will be rewarding. This is a way for all organizational types to see and feel what it will be like to work in an organized space. But perhaps the most important reason is because this will clearly show you what you actually use on your desk, and just how much of it you can do without. This small step will also impress clients and colleagues—or, at least, pique their curiosity.

Don't get me wrong—I am not asking or expecting you to have such a Spartan desktop on a regular basis. We all enjoy and need a little personality and warmth in our workspaces; such personal reminders help keep us focused and motivated, and they can humanize us to the world-at-large. Eventually, it will be OK to bring some of these items back, but not until you know what you truly need and use to do your job.

In addition to your computer and telephone, get a standard legal pad to use for notes that week. Each day, write the date at the top of the page, and start each work day with a new sheet. Use this pad in place of all other notes, including post-its. Use it in addition to any other portable devices you typically use. Carry it with you to meetings. For one week, experience a workspace with only the essentials. When you need to retrieve something from the box of desktop items, make a note of it on your legal pad and return the items to the box when you leave for the day. This information will become especially useful later.

Step Two: Make a Decision

At this point, you have had time to think about your organizational type, observe the styles of colleagues and friends, and experience an empty desk surface. Now, it's time to decide just how far you're willing to go. How does "clean" feel to you? Do you want to take this all the way, or do you think you don't have the time to make this sort of commitment?

I suspect that if you've read this far, you're willing to do what's necessary to get completely organized, but I am mentioning this now because this is truly the fork in the road, and I do not want you to feel like you have somehow failed if you do not follow every future step I've outlined in the rest of the book. The decision to become more organized is a personal one that will net many professional benefits, but it takes time, care, and commitment. It is possible to follow some of these steps or gradually do a complete overhaul. Really, any small step you decide to make is to be commended.

Change is never easy. In the following sections of this chapter, we will discuss what's necessary to completely change your workspace (or, at least, its contents), including weeding through what you will eventually decide to keep, toss, and archive. Once you have determined what there is to work with, we will spend the next two chapters on where to put it. Regardless of what you decide to do, I hope you will continue reading this chapter until skipping to the next.

Step Three: Weeding

We're not talking gardening here. Rather, this term concerns combing through every drawer, file, box, and piece of furniture to determine what you have to work with. Through this process, you will decide what to keep, toss, and archive. So, in a sense, this is a bit akin to gardening of the outdoor variety because this type of weeding can also be dirty and painful—but it looks great afterward (and must be kept up and maintained to stay that way).

It will take a lot of time to go through all of the items in your workspace, and it may have been months or years since you've seen some of this stuff. I even suggest thumbing through case files to make sure everything in them needs to be there. Whatever doesn't should be shredded, even if it's just a post-it note or an envelope. You never know what someone else might find useful to the detriment of your clients.

Most importantly, this is not a task to delegate to someone else. This is your space and your stuff, and no one else should know it better than you do. As you look through everything, sort it into a keep pile and use a large trash can for the toss pile. We'll get to archiving momentarily.

You might also find that some of the "toss" items (or even some of the "keeps") could be donated. But don't get distracted by these possibilities. Wait until you've completed the process. Be ruthless. If you haven't used these items in two years and they have no emotional, intellectual, or high monetary value, or you could easily replace them at little to no cost if you found you did need them (such as copies of articles and reports or internal documents of which someone else is holding the original), then toss them. Once you've finished the first go-around, do it again. You'll be amazed at how many of the items you initially kept can get tossed when reviewed a second time.

Once you've gone through this process a couple of times, revisit the idea of donations—or sales. Some of you may have law books that you don't use, need, or display that could be donated to law schools in the United States and abroad. As we all remember, these books are very expensive, and even an obsolete or heavily highlighted textbook could be cherished by someone else. You might also consider selling them to independent book buyers, many of whom will stop by your office to verify the current monetary value of the books, pay you cash, and haul them away. For names of reputable legal book dealers, contact professors at your local law school or contact local law libraries. These buyers routinely visit the halls of law schools looking for books to buy.

After you're satisfied with your decisions of what to keep and toss, it's time to give some serious thought to what you want to keep in your workspace. What in the keep pile do you really need to do your job effectively? What are you retaining for emotional reasons? If half or more of your keep items are more sentimental in nature than they are functional, it is important for you to really be honest with yourself about why they are there. As a general rule, no more than 25 percent of the items in your workspace should be personal or decorative—and that's on the high end. Ideally, you should aim for no more than 10 percent. Everything else should have a particular use or function to contribute to your work as an attorney.

It is possible—if not more efficient and personal—to insert your personality into ordinary, everyday work items. For example, you might choose an eclectic pen, a unique container for paperclips, or an interesting mouse pad. Make sure every item earns a spot in your workspace. Ordinary items can be functional and meaningful; together, they can work to give your workspace personality and style—and organization.

Potential Challenges in the Process

As you now know, weeding is not easy, and the challenges may vary depending on your organizational type. For example, Stackers may neatly place haphazard stacks into piles to sort through later, but "later" never seems to arrive. Spreaders may start mixing sorted items with items that need to be sorted, eventually having to start over. Free Spirits may have particular trouble taking too much time thumbing through interesting materials that have been rediscovered through weeding, and Packrats may have difficulty with deciding which mementos stay and go. Since work will continue to go on, cases and clients and colleagues will invariably cause multiple interruptions. Regardless of your organizational type, you may experience all of these challenges as you move through this process. But keep at it.

A Note about Hoarding

At first glance, the haphazard appearance of some offices, particularly those of Free Spirits and Packrats, may lead one to wonder whether there may be a problem with hoarding. "Compulsive hoarding is defined as 'the acquisition of, and failure to discard ...

possessions that appear to be useless or of limited value; ... living [or work] spaces sufficiently cluttered so as to preclude activities for which those spaces were designed; and ... significant distress or impairment in functioning caused by the hoarding.'"[2] However, in contrast to the tendencies of Free Spirits and Packrats, hoarders also collect garbage.[3] Furthermore, "[w]hat differentiates hoarders from people who are simply messy is that hoarders' living [and work] spaces can no longer be used as originally intended."[4] This disorder afflicts about five percent of the population.[5]

Keeping these facts about hoarding in mind, there may indeed be some attorneys who do fall into the hoarder category. Those who face this problem may need professional help that extends beyond the scope of this book.

Step Four: Creating an Archive

You've weeded through the items in your workspace and are left with a pile of keeps. But, of this pile, not everything needs to remain in your office. This is a challenge everyone continues to face on a daily basis, and it tends to be the cause of an organized space morphing back into a disorganized one. It is also a boon to the storage industry.[6] It is the challenge of keeping what you don't always use because you will eventually need it someday. This is where an archive comes in handy. The trick is to define it—and to follow the rules you create.

"Archive" is a noun and a verb. It is a thing and an activity. As a noun, the Oxford English Dictionary defines it as "a place in which

---

2. Keith P. Ronan, *Navigating the Goat Paths: Compulsive Hoarding, or Collyer Bros. Syndrome, and the Legal Reality of Clutter,* 64 RUTGER'S LAW REV. 235, 237-38 (2011).

3. *Id.* at 239.

4. *Id.* at 239–40.

5. *Id.* at 240.

6. The storage industry "generated more than $24 billion in annual U.S. revenues" in 2013. Self Storage Association, *2013 Fact Sheet,* www.selfstorage.org (accessed 3/23/15).

public records or other important historic documents are kept." As a verb, the same dictionary defines it as "to transfer to a store containing infrequently used files, or to a lower level in the hierarchy of memories." In essence, by creating an archive, you're defining what will always remain in your workspace, what is important enough to keep and store, and what will eventually be discarded.

You might be thinking, "It's not that serious," but it is. Until you define what stays and goes, anything goes and everything stays—which will lead to perpetual disorganization. Of the items in your keep pile, a good half of them can probably be archived. What, among your things, can be viewed as "historic" or "important" enough to store away for safe keeping? When and how would these items lose that designation?

The best way to start your archive is to go to a packaging or moving store and purchase a few clean, sturdy boxes. Create descriptions of what will be archived in each box, and keep a record of this in your office. Write the description and date on the box, sort items accordingly, and place them in the box. Then store them away in a closet or garage. Only rent a storage facility if it's absolutely necessary. Typically, if you're weeding and archiving on a regular basis (at least annually), a rented storage space should not be necessary.

Step Five: Working with the Keeps

You've sorted, weeded, tossed, and archived. Now, you should have a good amount of items left to work with. In the next chapters, we will discuss ways to place and keep them in your workspace, keeping in mind the needs of different organizational types. We will also discuss items you may want to consider adding to your workspace.

Chapter Checklist

✓ Take the questionnaire to determine your organizational type. The four organizational types are:
  - **Stacker**: Stackers tend to be visual and tactile and feel more in control when they have structure in their work surroundings.
  - **Spreader**: Also visual, Spreaders need to see everything they are working on at once. This can quickly become problematic when they are working on multiple projects.
  - **Free Spirit**: Free Spirits are idea lovers who tend to be heavily involved in one or two subjects, and they are less concerned about their surroundings than they are in their particular causes or subjects. They have an intellectual tie to the items in their workspaces.
  - **Packrat**: Packrats have emotional ties to their items and have trouble throwing anything away. They feel more comfortable with a lot of things around them. They are constantly filling in empty spaces.

✓ Start the organization process by:
  - Clearing Your Desk
  - Weeding
  - Archiving
  - Working with the Keeps

Any activity becomes creative when the doer cares about doing it right, or better.

John Updike

CHAPTER 2

OFFICE LAYOUTS

In recent years, many law firms around the country have been dramatically altering the style and feel of their spaces to become more modern and appealing to attorneys and clients alike.[1] Gone are the days when law firm décor was limited to dark woods, luxurious rugs, and stately grandfather clocks. (However, if that's your cup of tea, there is nothing wrong with that. In fact, some clients may continue to appreciate and expect it.) But an increasing number of firms and solo practitioners are taking bold steps to redefine what a law firm "should" look like in the 21st century.[2]

For example, many law firms are beginning to use angular architecture, exposed metals, lighter-toned woods, minimalist furniture, and large-scale works of art to create sleek workspaces with a decidedly modern feel.[3] Smaller firms and solo practitioners have successfully renovated Victorian homes and bank buildings with a playfully traditional flair.[4] One of the biggest trends concerns the use of open spaces, such as conference rooms, pods, flexible work areas (or "flex zones"), and "war" rooms where practice groups meet to prepare for battle.[5] Law firms are also trying to create spaces that encourage cross-pollination among attorneys special-

---

1. *See generally* Jill Schachner Chanen, *The New Office: Today's Interior Design Trends Promote Efficiency, Collegiality—Even Conservation*, ABA JOURNAL, July 2005. *See also* Steve Ginsberg, *Law Firm Décor Favors Simple Elegance*, EAST BAY BUSINESS TIMES, February 25, 2005; Jay Strother, *Space: Your Final Frontier*, LEGAL MANAGEMENT, April/May 2012.

2. *Id. See also* Marc G. Reynolds, CLM, *The Non-Hierarchical Law Firm*, LEGAL MANAGEMENT, October/November 2007.

3. *See* Chanen, *supra* note 1.

4. *Id.*

5. See Robert C. Mattern, *Maximize Your Office Design's Efficiency*, LEGAL MANAGEMENT, May/June 2008.

izing in different areas of law, while also creating spaces that exude a touch of class without being stodgy or ostentatious.[6] Above all else, the goals appear to be for firms to increase levels of comfort and confidence.[7] These two goals should also be mirrored in your personal workspace.

The concept of comfort rests on both sides of the table. Firms want attorneys to work in a comfortable environment because it is likely that many hours will be spent at the office, and the comfort of clients is crucial to their decisions to approach and return to a particular firm for legal assistance. Comfort does not mean sloppy. Much like our discussion of the word, "archive," in the previous chapter, "comfort" is both a noun and a verb. In the realm of legal professionalism, the concept of comfort puts everyone at ease to the extent possible, while also eliciting positive feelings that the work at hand can and will be done—and done well.

Setting the right tone also increases clients' confidence that they're working with attorneys with whom they can relate and who know what they're doing. A lawyer's reputation is a valuable asset, if not the most valuable. Your workspace is part of your reputation. In fact, it often makes the first impression. Securing the confidence of your clients is much easier to do when you're not explaining away a messy office. In contrast to misconceptions, some clients may not be impressed that you are "too busy" to clean your workspace; in fact, some may assume that you are either disorganized or too busy to handle their case and take their business elsewhere.[8]

Much like the canvas of a painting, the layout of your office is the foundation of your workspace. It concerns the size, format, and boundaries within which you must work to create a concept that inspires your own personal comfort and confidence. It also refers to furniture placement and how that can impact your space.

---

6. *Id.*

7. *See* Chanen, *supra* note 1.

8. *See, e.g.*, Wendy Werner, *Customer Service for Lawyers*, LAW PRACTICE TODAY, November 2006.

These concepts will be discussed in the following sections, along with recommendations for each organizational type.

Size

The concept of size concerns the physical area in which you're working. To determine the square footage, multiply the length of the space by its width. An increasing number of firms are decreasing the square footage of associates' and partners' offices for both financial and psychological reasons.[9] Offices of the same size are a great equalizer, and they lead to fewer moves associated with promotions. Instead, some firms have decided to simply treat new partners to nicer furniture instead of relocating them to the archetypical corner office. Some larger firms are decreasing office sizes so that no one has offices larger than 150 square feet, which is exactly 10 feet wide by 15 feet deep.[10] Some of you may see this as tiny, but this size offers many workable solutions for storage and, yes, comfort. Other offices are of the traditionally large variety, with furniture that can be rearranged to suit the inhabitant's particular needs and style. As you consider size, remember the heights of ceilings and the numbers of windows. Each can have an impact in what you store and how you store it. We will discuss some of those ideas in this chapter, and others in Chapter 4.

Format

This refers to the type of space in which you're working, or its classification. In other words, is it an office, a cubicle, a shared office, or an open space without walls? Although the vast majority of lawyers are assigned to offices—which is helpful for maintaining confidentiality due to the ability to close and lock the door to

---

9. *See* Strother, *supra* note 1 (discussing the trend toward more "modest" workspaces).

10. *See* Chanen, *supra* note 1.

protect sensitive information—a sizable minority of lawyers are assigned to cubicles and other spaces that lack privacy.[11] This is especially true of lawyers working in corporate environments.[12] The same is true for most judicial law clerks. Law students who work as clerks and paralegals working with attorneys also tend to work in cubicle settings. Despite their many drawbacks,[13] cubicles can offer a surprising array of organizational options, as we will discuss later in this chapter in the sections devoted to each organizational type. Those of you who must share an office or an open space will face unique challenges because you cannot completely control your workspace and are bound by the needs and tastes of another. Although this is not easy, it, too, is workable—especially if you have your own desk. For those who must share an office and a desk, many of the ideas in Chapter 8 will apply to you on a regular basis.

Boundaries

This concerns the potential obstacles or rules that might exist that could impact the decisions you make to alter your space. Is there any furniture affixed to the floors that cannot be moved? Are there built-in bookshelves or cabinets that you must work around? Where are the jacks for your computer and telephone? If you're working in an office, does every wall have a plug? If you're working in a cubicle, can anything be moved? How tall are the walls? Are you permitted to hang anything on the walls in your office or cubicle? What is the policy for bringing in items from home? Do you have an office decorating budget? What is the general feel of

---

11. *See* Daniel J. DiLucchio, *In-House Lawyers: Cubicles Versus Offices*, Altman-Weil, November/December 2004 (indicating that, although most lawyers work in offices, there are some corporate environments in which most or all attorneys work in cubicles).

12. *Id.*

13. For a comprehensive historical overview of cubicle design, *see* Julie Schlosser, *Cubicles: The Great Mistake*, FORTUNE, March 22, 2006.

the décor in common areas, and how much can you realistically stray from that look without a few words of opposition from the powers that be?

Furniture Placement

The best possible scenario is an office with movable furniture and few built-ins because this arrangement provides the most options for you to tailor the space to suit your particular organizational type. The placement of your furniture can work wonders for your space and for your psyche. Taking ownership of the space personalizes it, much like the choices you make in furnishing your home. As much as we don't like to think about it, lawyers probably spend more time in the office than they do at home, unless they happen to work out of the home. For that reason alone, it's important to feel comfortable there. The most challenging scenario involves cubicles with furniture that cannot be moved, but as you might imagine, there are ways to work within those parameters, too. Some may want to incorporate concepts of Feng Shui—based on Chinese rules of spatial harmony—into their workspaces. If so, there are many respectable guides that can be found in bookstores and libraries, but two keys to remember are to try to avoid a desk arrangement that puts your back to the door, and to develop a clean space that encourages positive energy, or Chi.

Typical Layouts

Like most office environments, law firms and other places that employ lawyers tend to err on the conservative side with office furniture layouts—including those firms with offices that boast cutting-edge designs and works of art that rival large modern museums. There are the usual desk, office chair, file cabinet, shelving unit, and guest seating. Some spaces will have extra pieces, such as a credenza or a small conversation area with a small table and chairs. Desks are often arranged in either an "L" or a "U" shape, and shelving can either exist in an overhead configuration over the desk, or there might be either bookshelves or built-in shelving on a separate wall. During the past several years, an increasing number of work environments are deciding to use furniture in the "P" shape, which is essentially a desk and conference table in one that was designed for increased flexibility of use—or at least that was the intention.[14] What often instead happens is that the round section at the end just becomes an extension of an already messy desk. In all of these scenarios, one or two file cabinets and a modest window complete the picture, although some spaces will have no windows.

Office Layouts by Organizational Type

In this section, we will discuss ways to maximize the layout of your workspace to best suit your organizational type. But please remember that moving your furniture is only part of the solution. We still need to address storage, stocking your desk (which will be covered in Chapter 3), and making sure you do your part to keep your space organized. If you have already decided what to keep and archive, which was discussed in Chapter 1, most of your furniture should be relatively empty and ready to move. If you haven't yet finished that step, you will still benefit from relocating any pieces that you can move to better suit your organizational type.

Stackers

Stackers work best in workspaces with a lot of nooks and crannies in which to neatly store and display books, reports, and other items. For those who are working in large law firms, you may either have built-ins over your desk and possibly also bookshelves and file cabinets to use as storage, along with either a desk and

---

14. *See* Karen Niemi, *The Death of Status: Office Design is Key to Employee Productivity and Client Satisfaction*, THE OREGON STATE BAR BULLETIN, December 2001.

conversation table, or a desk and table combination that is designed to serve both functions. Others may have little storage and primarily flat surfaces to work with. The main idea here is to create nooks in which to store items. However, as we discussed in Chapter 1, Stackers have a way of easily accumulating more stacks, so the challenge is to maintain awareness of what is being stored so that the amount of items does not accumulate into an uncontrollable heap instead of what the Stacker thought was simply a compilation of neat stacks. Because of this likelihood, Stackers might consider avoiding closed storage, such as credenzas, and instead use open storage, such as bookshelves and cubby holes. Every lawyer must deal with file cabinets, but this kind of closed storage can be limited to client files so that the Stacker is not tempted to squirrel away more neat stacks without dealing with them directly.

Spreaders

Spreaders need a lot of flat surfaces on which to work because they like to have room to spread out current projects. For this reason, a conference or meeting table in a Spreader's office may seldom, if ever, work out as planned because the Spreader will first cover his or her desk and then migrate over to the conference table for more space. However, Spreaders are very effective "Stackers" with items not in regular use. The best use of a Spreader's space is therefore vertical. They need to plan for as much vertical storage as possible, knowing that it will be used for storage only, and they must work very hard to avoid the temptation to spread from their desks to their conference table. For Spreaders whose offices are equipped with a desk/conference table configuration (which is better in theory than in practice for any organizational type), an effective way to create a wedge between what will be considered space to spread and room for conferencing is to insert what I like to call a gentle barrier. This could take the form of a series of books that are stacked vertically abutted on either side with nice bookends, a framed photograph or inspirational phrase, or a stately tray that holds business cards, a cup of pens, and a canister of paperclips.

Free Spirits

Free Spirits need places to store their items of interest so that they do not take over their workspace. In contrast to Stackers and Spreaders, Free Spirits greatly benefit from closed storage. A credenza or armoire would be ideal. Often, the items in a Free Spirit's office will get commingled with cases and other urgent work documents because they are directly relevant to the projects at hand, and to require a Free Spirit to stop collecting interesting items is unrealistic at best. Since many of the items will be based on a few key topics, the most efficient way to manage them is to group them by type instead of by topic. This grouping can take the form of "islands" in the Free Spirit's office, which are designated for different things. For example, a large basket could hold newspapers and magazines, and wayward reports could be harnessed in a credenza or an armoire. Books, in contrast, could be displayed openly, but by topic instead of in a haphazard fashion. For Free Spirits working in cubicles, one suggestion is to use one of the surfaces in your space to place two or three decorative baskets in which to group your things, and use the cabinets below for files and personal things that must be locked up when you leave for the day. For Free Spirits with conference tables, it would be wise to invest in a nice, large basket or container in which to quickly place items before meeting with clients, in case the table just happens to have a few items laying around.

Packrats

Like Free Spirits, Packrats benefit from closed storage and grouping. However, because they tend to prefer the full and cozy feel of a cluttered space, they also need some limited open storage. Large, flat surfaces should ideally be avoided because Packrats will always eventually fill them, and a full, flat space just does not look neat. Plus, Packrats like to see their collectibles and mementos. The best approach is to incorporate vertical storage for the grouping of collectibles that are interspersed with books, and also have some closed storage available for items that the Packrat wants nearby while maintaining a neat appearance for clients. Good furniture solutions for Packrats are attractive pieces that offer ample closed storage, and open vertical storage options for the many items the Packrat wants to actually see. Like Free Spirits, Packrats would also benefit from keeping one container around for a quick clean-up before clients arrive. However, it would need to be emptied on a regular basis so as not to become part of the ... regular décor. Since Packrats enjoy having things around them with personal meaning, one idea might be to try to incorporate furniture in your workspace with a particular meaning or emotional tie. Attorneys working in older, stately offices could use some family heirlooms, or those with more modern tastes could find personal comfort in having a piece in your office that was purchased on a shopping trip with someone you love. If it inspires positive memories, you are more inclined to use it—and to do so with care.

Getting the Picture

Descriptions are one thing, but as the old saying goes, "A picture speaks a thousand words." As you're planning your space, it may be very helpful for you to see examples of furniture and uses of space to help you rearrange your own. If you're a law student or a new lawyer with large loans and a small budget for this sort of thing, try ordering free catalogs from companies such as Pottery Barn, Crate & Barrel, and Restoration Hardware. All will send you beautiful catalogs free of charge, which are full of photos and ideas. Even if what's on the pages surpasses your budget, these images will provide ideas of what you can seek out on a more modest scale.

Chapter Checklist

✓ Measure the size of your office so that you know the square footage of the space you have to work with.

- Determine the format of your space. Are you working in an office, in a cubicle, a shared space, or an open space?
- Verify the boundaries in which you must remain as you make changes. In other words, are there official firm or company policies that you must follow when considering adding or moving furniture, or adding or removing anything from the walls?
- Assess the furniture layout of your office and the pieces that you have to work with. Will they meet the needs of your personal organizational type?
- Locate images of office layouts and furniture styles you like to guide you as you make changes to tailor your space to your needs and organizational type. Remember, it is possible to have a space that has a style that you like that also effectively meshes with the way you live and work among your things.

Then there's the joy of getting your desk clean, and knowing that all your letters are answered, and you can see the wood on it again.

Claudia "Lady Bird" Johnson

CHAPTER 3

DESK ARRANGEMENTS

Whether you've been practicing law for 30 years or are in your first year of law school, the one commonality all attorneys (and attorneys-to-be) share is the amount of time spent sitting at a desk. Our desks serve many purposes and functions—meetings with clients and colleagues, responding to e-mails, speaking on the telephone, reviewing files and cases, typing correspondence, eating meals and snacks, and supplying necessary storage. Despite technological advances, our desks continue to serve as the central location for all that we do.

Unfortunately, for as much time as we spend behind our desks, many of us are surrounded by spaces that are messy, cluttered, and inefficiently arranged.[1] This does nothing but work against us, cause additional stress, and lead to losses in revenue.[2] By some estimates, the average worker spends about an hour each day looking for misplaced items.[3] For attorneys, time literally is money. For that reason alone, a better organized desk is a wise investment.

---

1. However, desk disarray has not been a successful excuse or defense for attorneys or judges facing sanctions. *See, e.g.*, Nate Jenkins, *The Messy Desk Defense*, LINCOLN JOURNAL STAR, May 13, 2006; Michael Hoskins, *Justices Disagree on Judge's Penalty*, THE INDIANA LAWYER, March 12, 2009 (discussing the actions of a judge who was sanctioned for disorganized practices).

2. *See, e.g.*, J.J. McCorvey, *The Real Consequences of Office Clutter*, INC., January 29, 2010 (reporting on an Office Depot survey of 1,000 workers, resulting in a finding that disorganization led 47 percent to lose time, 16 percent to arrive late for meetings, and 14 percent to miss deadlines).

3. *See* Peg Tyro, *Clean Freaks*, NEWSWEEK, June 7, 2004 ("According to a study conducted by a Boston marketing firm, the average American burns 55 minutes a day—roughly 12 weeks a year—looking for things they know they own but can't find."); *see also Lost Something Already Today?* THE DAILY MAIL, March 20, 2012 (indicating that the most commonly misplaced items include keys, paperwork, purses, wallets, laptops, and tablets).

In Chapter 1, we discussed organizational types and began the process of creating an organized space. Regardless of the decision you made at that time to either go all the way with this or instead aim for a shorter distance of your choosing, it is good that you now at least know your organizational type. (If not, please take the Organization Questionnaire in Chapter 1 before going forward.) The first project we discussed involved clearing the top of your desk, living with an empty desktop for a week while using the removed contents out of a box adjacent to your desk, and keeping notes of what was used. Remember how I mentioned how that list would come in handy later? Well, later has arrived.

Although it may have been a bit uncomfortable to work on an empty surface and keep track of what you used all week long, the resulting list provides a priceless roadmap—one that will show you the way to knowing what to keep on your desk and what can be stored either in a desk drawer or in another section of your workspace. Most importantly, you experienced firsthand what you could live without and not miss. If you can do without something for a week, it does not need to take up valuable desk space.

No book for lawyers would be complete without the use of at least one hypothetical. We all have fond memories of hypos, don't we? (I know—neither do I.) As you may recall, the two items that you were permitted to keep on your desk during the empty desktop week were your computer and telephone (and a printer, if applicable), so they are not part of this list. (See Chapter 1, if a refresher is needed.) Hypothetically, let's say the items on your list included current files that require your attention, office supplies (such as a stapler, paper clips, and a highlighter), box of tissues, a mug, and the required pad and paper to jot down items you used from the box.

In Chapter 2, we discussed office layouts and suggestions for each organizational type. I briefly touched on a few of the most common desk configurations, including the "L" shape, "U" shape, and "P" shape. In this chapter, we will focus less on these particular shapes and more on how to stock them to your advantage. However, although we will not discuss shapes, we will address the issue of size. Therefore, this chapter will require the use of measuring tape.

Unless you're working on a flat surface, such as a table, your desk probably has at least one drawer. Most desks will have a drawer in the center and a combination of two small drawers and a bottom drawer for files on either side. Using these drawers to your advantage will free up valuable real estate on your desk's surface. Everything on top of your desk needs to be useful, functional, or decorative—in that order. The contents of your drawers should carry the same weight, but in more of a supporting role capacity. In legal terminology, the top of your desk should hold primary sources, while items stored inside of your desk are secondary sources. If your desk has either one or no drawer, you will need to limit yourself to housing primary sources there, and secondary sources in another part of your workspace that is close enough to reach in a pinch.

Back to the hypothetical. Of the list of items above, what should be classified as primary and what is secondary? What is useful, functional, or decorative? *The answers do not depend on the amount of space you have to work with.* That's the key. This is the point during which you set the rules that you will follow, no matter what. Otherwise, as previously stated, anything goes and everything stays and you'll soon be right back where you started.

Reviewing this list of items in order and thinking realistically, you've already established the importance of each of these items simply by using them daily for a solid week. But they are not all equally useful. Thinking in purely Orwellian[4] terms, some desk supplies are more equal than others. In other words, regardless of whether something is useful, functional, or decorative, it's up to you to create the rules that you will follow in the future for what stays and what goes. A good start would be to prioritize items based on their uniqueness or intrinsic value. What on this list could be classified as one-of-a-kind or something you could not find elsewhere or do without? Those are your primary materials. Anything else is secondary, at best.

---

4. This is a play on the famous quote from ANIMAL FARM, by George Orwell: "All animals are equal, but some animals are more equal than others."

So, the answer depends on you and your needs. As guidance, I will answer this question as though I were trying to decide what should be stored on top of and within my own desk. Current files would be classified as useful and functional, but I would have no more than three current files on my desk at a given time. I would likely have a basket or tray to hold these files. Office supplies and tissues are useful and functional, but I would place them in the top drawer because they are usually not decorative and they would take up too much space on the desktop. Before placing them there, I would measure the insides of the drawers and purchase inexpensive drawer organizer trays so that I could neatly store items in the various compartments instead of allowing them to float around to avoid the beginnings of a new junk drawer. It's amazing how these inexpensive trays can corral so many wayward items and keep them orderly indefinitely. They also appeal to every organizational type. If I could not fit the box of tissues inside of a drawer, I would place it on a conference table or within reach on a nearby credenza. The mug and the writing pad would stay on top of my desk. So, even though all of these items were used during the empty desktop week, I would store most of them inside of the desk instead of having them out in the open. I would then have room for other important items in an arrangement that I like to call the "System."

What Is the System?

The System is a way for you to set up the surface of your desk that you can use in any desk configuration and in any type of legal position for a modest cost. I have used this concept for years, and I have assisted others with similar set-ups, with great success. Although I designed it for lawyers, it has also worked for professionals working in other industries. It varies slightly based on organizational types, but using the System will help to keep your desk looking and feeling neat and orderly—even during those inevitable instances where you've fallen off of the organizational wagon.

The first step is to purchase a simple metal step file holder. Typically, desktop step files hold about eight letter-sized folders. Next, select a color for your letter-sized files that is different than any other colors of folders in your office. This color should be unique and tasteful because it will always be visible. Many office supply stores also offer folders with pleasant, muted designs, which could also be useful for this purpose. That way, this element would be useful, functional, and decorative—and also a way to sneak in a bit of your personality on your desktop. These eight folders will hold the various items on your desk that you need at a moment's notice, and other incidentals that invariably need a permanent home.

For these files, take some time to think about categories that will satisfy numerous needs. In the step file on my desk, I have a few regular categories, while the others have changed with positions I have held. The regular folder categories include the following: "Daily Work File," which is first in line in the step file and is designed to hold wayward items, such as mail I need to open; "Current Projects" for tasks that I am working on; "Reference" for lists with phone numbers, court addresses, and the index to the files in my file cabinets (more on this in Chapter 4); "Events" for those I plan to attend; and "Completed Projects" for anything that has been finished and needs to be filed. There are a few additional slots with folder titles that are relevant to what I am working on. One concerns course schedules, another is devoted to committees, and the final one is for this book. Other suggested labels include "Human Resources," "Staff," and "Notes."

As previously mentioned, we will discuss the filing system for the files in your filing cabinets in Chapter 4. At this point, we are focusing on the files that will be stored in your step folder. If you're using this System correctly, there are two space-wasters that can and should be avoided at all costs: the in and out boxes. Think about it—have you ever seen a successful in and out box system that lasted longer than a few days?

No, contrary to popular opinion, in and out boxes are a complete waste of time. They are not part of the System for a reason— they don't work for any organizational type. Stackers will keep them stacked as high as possible before the stacks eventually topple over, Spreaders will eventually lose them in the shuffle of other papers, Free Spirits will allow piles of interesting-looking periodicals to languish unopened, and Packrats will eventually treat them like the rest of the scenery. So, get rid of your in and out boxes. They're great in theory, but on a daily basis they will create nothing but a messy space. Instead of using these useless boxes, have people put items face down on your chair instead. That way, you will be forced to handle your mail and place items in the relevant folders in your step file without the extra steps involved with using an in and out box.

Chapter Checklist

✓ Review the list of items that you repeatedly used during the empty desktop week to determine what you need to store on and in your desk.

- Measure your desktop and the insides of your drawers to determine the amount of space you have to work with.
- Purchase and use inexpensive trays to keep your drawers tidy and to prevent loose items from moving around, thereby creating new "junk" drawers.
- Ensure that everything on your desktop is useful, functional, or decorative—in that order.
- Set guidelines for primary and secondary resources. Primary resources belong on the surface of your desk, while secondary ones are stored in drawers. For those who are working in desks without drawers, store your secondary resources away from your desk.
- Purchase a step file holder and unique folders to create and use the System.
- Eliminate "in and out" boxes.

Anything you lose automatically doubles in value.

Mignon McLaughlin

Chapter 4

Paper and
Electronic Files

Times have changed since the days when files were kept in one format. In the not-too-distant past, files consisted of sheets of paper held in a legal-sized folder; typically, everyone shared one master copy. Although attorneys continue to maintain records in this traditional print format, they must also now keep track of myriad electronic files, which have become equally important to a successful practice. However, these files are often kept in multiple copies and versions, which can also include a variety of updates and revisions, and which may not match the contents of the version in print. It is therefore crucial to develop methods to maintain personal print and electronic files in your office, as well as devise a way to make sure these methods can be easily understood by others.

In an additional modern development, the legal field now has as much turnover as other professions, and lawyers routinely inherit files from other lawyers.[1] As a result, facilitating the ability of other lawyers to hit the ground running will do nothing but enhance your reputation. Clients will also feel a heightened sense of importance that their materials are handled with such foresight and care. Although some firms have guidelines in place for file maintenance and management, the best plan of attack is to follow any rules that may already exist, while also having a clear and con-

---

1. The National Association of Law Placement (NALP) estimates that, based on a national study from 2006 to 2011 that comprised more than 22,000 associate hires and 17,000 associate departures, nearly 75 percent of associates left their positions within five years. *See Keeping the Keepers III: Mobility & Management of Associate Talent*, NALP, February 2014.

sistent way for anyone to be able to locate important information in your absence. Like other types of organization we have discussed, this, too, will take a lot of thought.

If you completed all of the tasks outlined in Chapter 1, you have already weeded through your paper files and decided what to keep, toss, and store in an archive, and you have shredded unneeded sensitive documents. You will also need to repeat these steps electronically to weed through your e-mails to decide what to keep, toss, and archive. Even if you have not yet started or completed any of these tasks, reading this chapter will help to get you started in your plans to organize materials in both formats.

We will focus on the process of organizing your files in print and electronic versions so that you can develop methods for keeping them tidy that mesh best with your personal organizational type. Notice, I called this a *process* because you are developing *customized* guidelines that you know that *you personally* can and will stick with indefinitely. In contrast to this process, anyone can spend long hours cleaning their workspace just once (or having someone else do it), but doing so without a plan to keep it that way will quickly get you right back where you started. This is a process that will require you to be honest with yourself so that you can make adjustments now so that you will have an easier time maintaining your workspace on a daily basis. Therefore, when you're making plans for your space, focus less on how you would like to be and more on how you realistically are.

As you're reading, if it seems like I am asking a lot of questions, you'll be correct. As I have mentioned, the organizational process takes time, thought, and honesty. The actual act of physically altering your space can otherwise have no staying power. As you review the various questions, it is vital that you take the necessary time to really think about how you react in various situations throughout the day. Also, realistically think about how frequently you will be willing to do what's necessary for upkeep. If done properly, most of the work of maintaining an organized filing system is done on the front end. This means that if you plan properly and are willing to roll up your sleeves from time to time, your space can remain organized with relatively minimal effort.

As a disclaimer, I do not profess to be a software expert, but brief mentions of a few commonly used programs and devices will be sprinkled throughout this discussion. By mentioning them, I am neither recommending nor criticizing them. They will instead solely be used for conversational purposes. There are many brands of software and gadgetry that you can employ to assist you in these efforts, and each will offer slightly different bells and whistles. In theory, what they have in common is a way for you to retrieve what you need as quickly as possible, while saving paper and space. Again, there are no wrong answers. Any program or tool is only wrong if it doesn't work for you. As additional idea, you might also consider asking someone who shares your organizational type for suggestions.

Organizing Paper Files

I don't know anyone who enjoys filing, but most of the people I have met tend to like (or at least appreciate) files that are well organized. Even the Packrats among us can't help but admire organized files. They look neat and orderly, and it is comforting to know that everything is where it belongs. It's just a question of getting there—and doing what it takes to keep it that way.

But what, exactly, is an organized file? As Stackers well know, it takes more than a neat grouping of papers to achieve true organization. For our purposes, an organized paper file may be defined as one for which you have designated a name and have consistently placed anything tangentially related to this topic together in one folder. It is also one that you can assume with great certainty will have what you're looking for simply because of its name. Some of you may prefer to institute a particular format within your files so that you will not have to do much digging to find what you're looking for, while others will be satisfied with the knowledge of an item's general whereabouts within a particular file. Regardless of which method you choose, it's important that you develop a concept that you will realistically follow on a consistent basis—so consistently, in fact, that it becomes a habit that you and others can depend on.

As you develop your personal filing system, think about how you work on a daily basis. What's the first file-related thing you do when you arrive in the morning? Do you bring files home with you? Besides papers, what else will be placed in the files? How often will you weed through files to keep them clean and well managed, and where will items be archived? Do you leave files open on your desk while you're working on them? Will you put them away when you're finished with them, or let them stack up on a table or chair? Do you have file cabinets in your desk and in your workspace? How do you use them? Finally, what types of files do you use and need—those for clients, personal files, and others based on legal topics, or a combination of the three?

In addition to the files stored in your desk, file cabinets, and other locations, there are also those that may rest on your desktop that do not have a permanent home. What do you leave on your desk that could or should be placed in file folders in the interest of privacy, or simply to keep your desktop clean and tidy? We discussed incorporating the System for desktop files in the previous chapter, so many wayward items that once sat on your desktop may now have a home in your new step file holder. However, many of you will probably also keep case files on your desk while you're working on them. For files on your desk without a permanent home, designate a place for them inside or near your desk. If they're close to you, they are probably important. As their importance decreases, move them to spaces at a greater distance away from your desk. Anything closest to where you sit at the computer should be of the utmost importance. Otherwise, you will constantly be looking for things all over your office. If you've already begun the process of clearing out the drawers in your desk, you might consider using one of them for the most important current projects—especially if they would take up too much space on your desk or are chock-full of sensitive materials.

Another suggestion is to introduce color-coding into your personal filing system. This works well for all organizational types. As a caveat, the any file colors you choose should differ from the color you have chosen for the System on your desktop. For example, the files on your desktop could be forest green or lavender (*i.e.*, colors that mesh with many decors and will not seem unprofessional, but are not typically used for official legal files), while client files could be red, and other files could be yellow. This way, when your eyes scan the desk or any other surface that may have files—including stacks—you will have a quick and easy way to get a general idea of what's there without having to dig through it. For those of you whose firms use only manila or green folders, you could still use personal colors for files in your office, and use post-it notes of colors matching your personal filing system to stick on folders while they are in your workspace.

Once you've completed this process, type up a master file list and keep it in the "Reference" folder in the step file on your desktop. This list will include colors, titles, and locations of file folders. That way, anyone who might need to locate a file in your absence will at least have a general idea of where to look. It will also make you look incredibly organized—and thoughtful.

Organizing Electronic Files

Electronic files may not take up the same amount of physical space in your office, but they can still benefit from being properly maintained and stored. On average, many attorneys receive more than 100 e-mails each day.[2] Furthermore, despite the proliferation of alternative methods of electronic communication, e-mail is still the most commonly used format for business communications.[3] Although some of this can be classified as junk or spam, deleting it still takes seconds of precious time away from handling the messages that matter. These moments can add up. Even if only five minutes a day are wasted on useless e-mails, this results in 1,825 minutes in a year—which is a little over one full day. One minute

---

2. *See* Thomas Rowe, *Boon or Bane? Eliminating Email Overload in Law Firms*, CONSTRUCTION LITIGATION, September 22, 2014.

3. *Id.* ("Recent statistics from 2013 show that 100 billion business emails were sent each day and that the rate will continue to grow around 7–8 percent per year.")

each day of wasted time totals just over six hours in a year. One second each day? About 10 minutes.

But we all know that e-mail never takes just a second, and we all have several software programs that we use on a daily basis. This doesn't even take into account all of the external programs that must also be used because of the requirements of entities outside of our workplaces, such as those that must be used to complete electronic filings on the websites of various courts, as well as various case management systems and programs to design supporting documents to use during presentations and trials.

So, there are filing needs for e-mail, documents, images, cases, articles, correspondence, presentations, websites, and countless other materials—and all in a variety of programs and formats. Additionally, you may need to save various versions of some of these documents in furtherance of your cases. Moreover, many of us also have personal e-mail addresses through free resources associated with popular Web search engines. All of this needs to be corralled into a virtual, yet tangible, system that will enable you to find what you're looking for and keep what you need.

One idea is to create a system that mirrors your paper files, or closely resembles it, so that you can keep track of various materials in an electronic format in case you need them. You would then only print documents on paper when necessary, and a master document list could easily be generated to insert in the paper folder to make the file complete. The challenge with this system is with upkeep. It sounds great, but who, realistically, has the time to do all of this while also keeping track of the various projects that require immediate attention? At the end of the day when you're so tired that all you want to do is drag yourself out of the office, pick up a bite to eat, and go home to relax, could you really picture yourself spending an extra half an hour scrolling through your e-mails and documents to ensure everything was filed correctly in every electronic folder? If you can, this is a great system, but if you cannot, then I have another suggestion: Keep it simple. Instead of mirroring your paper files, instead create files based on topical areas, with additional subtopic files based on dates. For example, you could use either a "noun" or "verb" approach: people, places, things, and activities. Within each of these folders, you could have subfolders for dates or years. The most important thing is to create a system that works for you, and that you will use consistently—and which will not take too much effort to maintain.

With electronic files, you have the luxury of relatively limitless space—unless you are bound by constraints imposed by your employer, equipment, or both. Regardless, you still have more space to work with than you do in your physical workspace. As a result, there's less pressure to maintain the same disciplined upkeep as is necessary with your workspace. Since you have more space to work with, you might consider imposing a requirement to spend five minutes per day on electronic upkeep. Remember, as we have discussed, five minutes a day adds up to just over a day per year—and spending just one day each year maintaining your electronic files will produce countless dividends for you every day, regardless of your position.

Organizing Paper and Electronic Files by Organizational Type

As is the case with other elements of developing and maintaining an organized workspace, each organizational type will have strengths and weaknesses with managing their paper and electronic files.

Stackers may appear to have neater spaces because they tend to place everything in orderly piles; however, as their projects increase, so will the number of stacks. They may delay filing and instead create a stack of items that need to be filed, or they may amass a few such stacks if they're especially busy. However, they will eventually dutifully go through their stacks because of their visual and tactile natures. The main challenge Stackers will face with paper filing is limiting themselves to one pile of items to be filed at a given time. As for electronic filing, Stackers may tend to keep a larger number of folders than most types because compartmentalizing information provides them a sense of comfort and control. This is fine, as long as the Stacker remembers all file names and locations.

Spreaders will keep files neatly stored—until they need them. Spreaders are highly visual, and are the most likely to work with files spread out and opened on their desks or other work surfaces. The main challenge Spreaders will face is keeping one file open at a time. The primary challenge with electronic filing concerns the inbox. Spreaders tend to use too few personal folders, and have enormous inboxes that must be waded through at a given time. This type would benefit from creating additional folders to lessen the visual overload of wading through hundreds or thousands of messages that have already been read.

Free Spirits will be far more likely to work at maintaining their files if they can somehow make the task interesting. Otherwise, files will be placed in stacks and piles among the various books and magazines that are in the spotlight at a given time. They also need to limit the number of files that are permitted in their workspaces, including those that they are currently working on. Everything cannot be of equal importance. It will therefore be important to prioritize. As for electronic filing, the greatest challenge Free Spirits face is the problem of "out of sight, out of mind." Therefore, it will be important for them to schedule small segments of time to revisit files to see what's there, what's still needed, and what may be discarded.

Packrats must find an emotional motivation for keeping their paper filing under control. Since many of the items around them have personal ties, there must be an even stronger motivating factor than the items, themselves, that encourages them to toe the organizational line. It could be tied to their reputation or the feelings of someone they care about and want to keep happy. Whatever it is, it must have staying power in order to keep the Packrat motivated to continue to make the effort to keep his or her space as tidy as realistically possible. Electronic filing is much less of a challenge, simply because any messes are limited to the confines of the computer and are not visible to anyone but the user. But just because no one else sees them does not mean they do not need regular maintenance. When creating electronic files, Packrats would be advised to keep the names as simple and general as possible in order or keep the number of files and references to a minimum—which will make items easier to locate in the future.

Chapter Checklist

✓ Weed through your paper and electronic files to determine
  what to keep, toss, and archive.
  - Think about how you work on a daily basis. What will you
    realistically do to maintain your paper and electronic files?
  - Check to see whether your employer has guidelines in place
    for how paper files are to be handled and maintained.
  - Introduce color-coding into your personal filing system to
    help you locate what you need more quickly and effi-
    ciently. You can also use color-coding with files that are
    not permanently stored in your office by using post-it
    notes in corresponding colors.
  - Create an electronic filing system that uses simple terms,
    and schedule five minutes each day to keep it tidy and
    maintained.
  - Address potential challenges based on your organiza-
    tional type.

Half the times when men think they are talking business, they are wasting time.

Edgar Watson Howe

Chapter 5

Financial Recordkeeping

Unless you're a tax lawyer, chances are you are more of a "words" person than a "numbers" person. In fact, the absence of math classes may have been part of the allure of going to law school. It was for me—assuming, of course, that law school can be considered alluring. Regardless of this potential preference for the written and spoken word over anything classified as mathematical, all lawyers and lawyers-to-be have some sort of financial recordkeeping expectations. If you're a law student, there are student loans, tuition, and school supplies. If you're practicing at a large firm, there are billable hours, receipts, and expense accounts. If you're a solo practitioner, there are all of the responsibilities of running a business—while also practicing law. Unless you have an MBA or are also a CPA, it's easy to get overwhelmed with all of the financial obligations that require your attention. Even if you have an accountant on the payroll to handle your affairs, it is important to have a general knowledge of your finances, and most clients will appreciate it. This chapter will focus on ways to take control of all of the financial records you may have to handle by using methods that are the most likely to keep you organized while doing so.

Lawyers are given great responsibilities with respect to their clients and the legal profession, so it is surprising that this topic is seldom, if ever, included in the required law school curriculum. Although this subject is often covered in Law Office Management classes, the class is usually an elective course. Although legal ethics and the importance of accurate recordkeeping are addressed in the Professional Responsibility courses required by all law schools, the nuts and bolts of just how to do this on a daily basis seldom receive much attention. But it seems that if more law students knew what they were getting themselves into, they would be better prepared to handle these financial responsibilities in practice. Maintaining good records is an acquired skill, but it is one that clients expect us to know right out of law school. Instead, many of us learn as they we go along—which can be challenging for all concerned.

Many of the transgressions associated with financial *faux pas* can be traced back to disorganization. Examples include commingling of funds, billing errors, and a failure to meet filing deadlines (including those for business and income taxes). Any of these actions could lead to public reprimands or, in the most severe of cases, disbarment. At the very least, these errors will damage client confidence and satisfaction, thereby decreasing new and repeat business in the future. Word of mouth travels fast, so you might as well do everything you can to ensure it moves in your favor.

This chapter will be divided into sections discussing the areas commonly needing the most attention—Billable Hours, Expenses, Accounts, and Record Management. Interspersed through the sections will be recommendations for various organizational types.

As was the case in Chapter 4, I must insert a brief disclaimer about software. There are a variety of excellent programs available for maintaining financial records, and I encourage you to try them, if that's your preference. But even the most technologically savvy lawyers are battling disorganization, so there must be a point between information gathering and data entry that is falling through the cracks. If I mention a program, it will be for conversational purposes only and should not be viewed as an endorsement or a criticism. As I have previously suggested, you might also consult with someone who shares your organizational type for recommendations of programs to incorporate into your practice.

Billable Hours

One would be hard pressed to find anyone who enjoys the task of recording and maintaining billable hours.[1] Who wants to keep track of every moment of the workday in six-minute increments? Unfortunately, the dreaded billable hour appears to be here to stay at most firms, so the best plan of attack is a good offense. Even if this is not required, it is wise to keep solid work records. It is much easier to establish a method for keeping track of your work as you go along than it would be to try to remember what you accomplished when it's too late to do so accurately. The challenge is in determining the best times to stop what you're doing to record your time. It almost seems counterproductive to stop working to record what you have already done. In a sense, it almost seems like a waste of time to spend time recording your time—especially when that time might be better spent working. Although there are a few firms that are trying alternative billing methods, this discussion will focus on billable hours in the traditional sense because the vast majority of firms still use this system.[2]

The typical billable hour system requires attorneys to bill their time in six-minute increments. Only times during which attorneys are actively involved in tasks related to a case may be counted. Other times, such as trips to the break room for another cup of coffee, chats in the hallways with a powerful partner, or a quick visit to the restroom, may not be counted. So, hypothetically, let's say you're drafting a memo that takes three hours to complete, and you start the project at 4:00 p.m. At 5:30, you have to leave the office to pick up your cleaning before the dry cleaner closes, and then you run into a colleague at the coffee shop on the corner and decide to stop and chat for a few minutes. It is now 6:15, which

---

1. Christine Parker and David Ruschena, *The Pressures of Billable Hours: Lessons From a Survey of Billing Practices Inside Law Firms*, University of Saint Thomas Law Journal, Fall 2011.

2. Stuart L. Pardau, *Bill, Baby, Bill: How the Billable Hour Emerged as the Primary Method of Attorney Fee Generation and Why Early Reports of its Demise May Be Greatly Exaggerated*, Idaho Law Review, 2013.

means that you have spent 90 minutes on the memo and have another 90 to go. So, you either hunker down for another 90 minutes at the office, which means you do not leave until 8:00 (and that assumes there were no interruptions within that time), take the work home to finish (where there could be additional interruptions), or do a little more, leave, and start fresh the next day. How are you going to keep track of your time for this and other projects while maintaining a life outside of work—and fulfilling the typical requirement of roughly 1,800 to 2,400 billable hours per year?

Keeping track of one's time is not just a matter of entering numbers into a software program, or delegating that task to an assistant or a paralegal. The most cumbersome aspect of this requirement falls somewhere in between the work, itself, remembering what was done, and keeping track of how much actual time was spent doing it. So, it is important to have a system in place that can be used before the hours are entered electronically.

The best way to handle this is to keep the system simple and repetitive, and to associate it with another daily activity that is often done when one is not billing time. I therefore suggest keeping a small notepad with you at all times that you can pull out during meals to record any time you've worked thus far that day. Most people eat at least twice daily, and jotting down tasks and time should take no more than five minutes each time, since no more than four or five hours will have elapsed since the last time you recorded your hours that day (assuming you do so at lunch and dinner). If a meal is a working meeting that can be billed, add it with the other time you record after the meal. If you're eating at your desk while working, record the time when you've finished eating. Since it is unlikely that you will spend every meal in working meetings, and you have to eat, this is a great way to still maintain productivity during a non-billable time. You will then also have a secondary resource in the notepad to have as a cross-reference for time entered in the system online that will be used to submit bills to clients. As you fill notebooks, add the start and end dates on the cover and archive them in your office.

For law students who will soon become lawyers, billable hours can offer a rude awakening to the business aspect of the practice of law. While in law school, there are numerous projects and deadlines, not to mention final exams, but no one is keeping track of the exact amount of time you are spending on successfully completing these tasks. Even if you're working while in school, it is highly unlikely that you are going to be expected to bill your time, although keeping track might be required for some clinical courses. To get a feel for what this is like, try keeping track of your time for a week. Count class time and time spent studying and working on assignments, and remember to eliminate any times not spent on the study of law in your record. Since it is more likely than not that you will need to record your billable hours once you graduate and start practicing law, it's better to know what will be expected of you and how to handle it before it becomes a required chore.

Expenses

On a given day, attorneys have a variety of financial obligations that are both professional and personal in nature. But, unlike other fields, sometimes it can be especially challenging to separate the two and keep them that way. Some expenses are obviously related to one's practice, including operating costs, filing fees, and memberships in professional organizations, such as the state and local bar associations. However, with client development becoming an increasingly expected part of a lawyer's daily—or at least regular—activities, it is not as easy to separate business from pleasure. The costs associated with attending events, taking prospective clients to lunch and dinner, and traveling for social occasions that could lead to new business are all expenses that might qualify as legitimate business expenses. (More on this topic will be discussed in Chapter 10.) Additionally, more mundane daily expenses, such as dry cleaning, gas, or a cup of coffee on the way to work, also need to be monitored so that you know how much you're spending and where. And, with the use of credit and bank cards instead of cash, receipts tend to accumulate at rates that often surpass the ability to make a record of them before they pile out of control. Electronic receipts can also create virtual "piles" that can be inconvenient and overwhelming to search through.

Some attorneys jot down notes on the backs of receipts to remind themselves of how the expense should be recorded. This can be very effective, provided the receipts don't pile up and become so voluminous that sitting down to officially record them becomes too burdensome of a chore. Also, like post-it notes, these receipts can get lost among the rubble if they are not properly managed and stored. However, if you're disciplined, this is an effective method. But please note that it requires perpetual consistency and diligence. Realistically, will you keep this up when you are stressed and busy?

If you know the answer is "no" and you won't keep this up, you might instead try either recording your expenses at the end of the day or filing receipts in your planner, if you've decided to use an organizer in a paper format.[3]

Yet another option is to keep your receipts in envelopes and to write the weekly dates on each one to record weekly. To maintain your receipts electronically, you may want to keep a spreadsheet to update on a regular basis. If you would prefer not to keep your receipts and feel more comfortable shredding them, you might consider scanning them online so that you can retain copies of the originals while also preserving valuable space in your office and at home. You can also share these files with your assistant, or your accountant, should you choose to hire one.

Accounts

Commingling of funds continues to be one of the most common reasons that lawyers are reprimanded and disbarred.[4] It essentially involves the wrongful use of money that should be solely associated with clients for an attorney's personal benefit. Al-

---

3. For a discussion of the use of paper versus electronic organizers, *see* Chapter 6.

4. For an historical overview, *see* Paul S. Gillies, Esq., *The Great Falls: A Survey of the Regulation of the Profession of Law 1778–2013*, Vermont Bar Journal, Fall 2013.

though there are lawyers out there who commit this offense due to either a lack of integrity or an abundance of financial desperation or greed, there are others who fall into this trap due to a lack of organization.

The best way to avoid combining funds into a jumbled and confusing financial mess is to keep them simple—and separate. Initially, it may feel cumbersome to maintain separate accounts, but it is ultimately the simplest way to keep your finances clear and separate. To take this approach a step further, I recommend having three accounts, each at a different bank. That way, your personal account is at one bank, your account for firm-related expenses is in an account at a second bank, and all client-related monies are reserved for a third. Regardless of whether you're practicing at a large firm or are a solo practitioner, this approach will save you time in poring over bank statements to cross-reference expenses because they will automatically be classified by the three banks. To avoid confusion, client development expenses would be paid through the "firm" account, and the "client" account would then be reserved for any revenue from clients; many firms already have such accounts, which are typically trust accounts, but I am instead referring to individual attorneys.

Even if you're working for a firm or another entity, keeping your expenses separate is an effective and definitive way to demonstrate at a moment's notice that you know and care very deeply about where your expenses belong, and it shows that you are making an intentionally public effort to ensure that your financial records are above reproach. To save space, you could maintain all three accounts online and keep statements in a folder on your hard drive. Many banks will also send an annual report with a breakdown of your expenses by category, as will credit card companies. This is especially true of business accounts. As a back-up, it would also be wise to save your statements onto a thumb drive and store this information in your desk. If you have a personal e-mail account and feel comfortable storing sensitive records there, you could forward copies there, too, as a second back-up.

Record Management

With all of the receipts, bank and credit card statements, and monthly bills from a variety of sources, it's easy to allow these print and electronic materials to quickly pile up. But what do you actually need to retain, and for how long? Your firm or company may have policies and procedures in place for the duration of time and acceptable formats for such record retention, but, if not, it is important for you to personally determine rules that will work best for you and that also comply with the highest standards imposed by both the legal profession and general good business practices. For guidance on records you are legally required to retain, there are many good reference materials and accountants to consult. This section will address ideas for the best methods for arranging the ones you decide to keep and purge based on your organizational type.

Stackers have a tendency to squirrel away items and feel that they are maintaining an organized space as long as items are grouped together. With receipts and statements, this can become problematic if the Stacker does not go through the stacks on a regular basis. I have known of Stackers who had a year's worth of receipts arranged in envelopes or in a shoe box, and the volume crept up on them because they thought they were organized just by keeping things sorted by type. Therefore, the greatest challenge this type faces is knowing when to purge, and doing so on a regular basis.

Spreaders, Free Spirits, and Packrats can easily lose items if they do not designate a place for them and adhere to it. Spreaders, in particular, can lose these important documents among the spread of items currently in progress on their desk or conference table. It is therefore important for all three of these types to designate spaces for these items that cannot be used for any other purpose. Like Stackers, they, too, will need to designate times to purge materials in regular intervals.

Chapter Checklist

✓ Maintaining good records is an acquired skill, but it is one that clients expect us to know right out of law school. Instead, many of us learn as they we go along—which can be challenging for all concerned.

- Establish good practices for billable hours, expenses, accounts, and record management to increase client confidence and satisfaction.
- Keeping track of one's time is not just a matter of entering numbers into a software program, or delegating that task to an assistant or a paralegal. The most cumbersome aspect of this requirement falls somewhere between the work, itself, remembering what was done, and keeping track of how much actual time was spent doing it. So, it is important to have a system in place that can be used before the hours are entered electronically.
- To get a feel for what it will be like to work with billable hours, law students should try keeping track of their time for a week.
- Keep accounts simple and separate to avoid commingling funds.
- Develop personal systems for record management, designate places to retain records in your office and online, and purge regularly so that items do not pile up.

Better three hours too soon than a minute too late.

William Shakespeare

Chapter 6

Planners and Electronic Organizers

Law school prepared us to be comfortable with the skills necessary for using a planner or an electronic organizer. If you graduated after 1990, the experience taught you to rely on heavy books that you had to carry, reference, and flip through in class, *and* you also had access to online tools for research and were expected to flip through screens with ease. Those of you who graduated during times when lawyers had no choice but to Shepardize cases in book format may be accustomed to using paper, but are possibly even more attracted to the ease of electronic organizers because they're different and new.

Thus far, we have discussed methods for organizing and storing the paper and electronic files that you keep in reference to clients and other business needs. These files are either stored in your workspace or in an archive, but they are not designed to be toted everywhere *en masse* on a daily basis. In contrast, this chapter will focus on the organizer you choose to keep with you throughout the day. Regardless of the type of law you practice, or whether you are working in a firm, as a solo practitioner, or in a government or corporate setting, you will need to use an organizer. This is also true for law students. We all need a plan to know where we're going. As the wise saying goes, "Failures don't plan to fail; they fail to plan."[1]

---

1. Harvey MacKay, syndicated columnist and motivational speaker. Accessed at www.successories.com (March 24, 2015).

Regardless of all of the personal planning resources currently available, some people still have a preference for using paper, and that's fine. Others may strongly prefer the small size, light weight, and convenient portability of an electronic device. The key is to choose the method that works best for you. Although this chapter offers comparisons between paper and electronic organizers, some of you may opt to use both simultaneously for different purposes. For example, you may want to have a paper organizer with you in meetings to jot down information and to take notes, but you may also want to have an electronic organizer handy to access e-mails or to locate the reference of an applicable statute or case. Conversely, you may want to figure out which one to choose to use for all functions.

Instead of including all of the most commonly used brands of paper planners and electronic devices, I will instead describe various features to consider that each has to offer. My rationale is admittedly practical: I am doing so in order to keep this information as current as possible for as long as possible. There will always be new resources on the market, but they will all likely offer similar features. Time will impact the efficiency of use more than the actual features themselves. Whether you're reading this in 2015 or 2050, it is important that you are aware that I have written this book with the needs of all current and future attorneys in mind, no matter the decade.

Even if you already own and use a paper or electronic organizer, this chapter will help you to decide whether you're currently using the best format for your needs, or if you might want to make a few adjustments. In the following sections, we will discuss the elements of each format, along with their pros and cons, as well as suggestions for each organizational type.

The Pros and Cons of Using a Paper Organizer

Paper organizers, or planners, as they are often called, are designed to do just that—to serve as a personal tool to help you to organize and plan your day. Some would take this a step further by instead saying that these tools help to plan our lives. From my communications with lawyers and law students, it seems that many like to keep "to do" lists, and planners are ideally suited to this method of keeping track of tasks that need your attention.[2]

Planners have existed in some form for centuries, and planners as we know them were developed by a lawyer.[3] They can be tailored to the tastes of the user in size, content, format, color, and function. They are typically less expensive than electronic devices, unless you're choosing an eel skin cover and paper made of 100 percent cotton. Every company that sells planners offers different sizes, and various styles of paper and calendars and note sheets to enable the user to mix and match, and an increasing number are offering packages based on various personal, professional, and life goals. There are "to do" lists and tabs and storage containers that enable you to archive your materials annually. Some offer calendars that begin mid-year, and others offer templates to customize items to print and include on your home or office computer.

Although planners are more of a traditional choice than an electronic organizer, they keep your information intact and the information can only be lost if you misplace your planner. Unlike an electronic organizer, planners do not "crash" or have memories that max out. If you need more "memory," simply add more paper. It is also easier to write on paper than it is on a small screen, the latter of which is often harder to read and requires uncanny thumb dexterity. Although in the past it used to be difficult to switch from brand to brand because of the numbers of holes in the sheets that were used would vary, now there is enough overlap to use items from various companies in the same planner.

---

2. For a pleasant article about the joys of using paper planners, *see* Terri Sapienza, *Daily Planners: Paper or Electronic?* THE WASHINGTON POST, January 4, 2012. *But see* Pamela Paul, *A Paper Calendar? It's 2011*, THE NEW YORK TIMES, July 29, 2011.

3. For a fascinating overview of the history of planners, *see Organizing Time*, National Museum of American History, http://americanhistory.si.edu/ontime/expanding/organizing.html (accessed March 24, 2015) (providing an overview of the "Lawyer's Day" prototype, created by Morris Perkin, an attorney who "joined with Dorney Printers to form Day-Timers, Inc.").

Also, as previously mentioned, costs can range from a reasonable $10 to upwards of $1,500, so there are planners in every price range. This price flexibility also enables users to try many types without breaking the bank.

Ironically, the planner may not be as sleek as a handy little gadget, but it can be easier and faster to find information. In the time it takes to turn on the device, you can open your planner and find the tab and pages you're looking for. Reading a sheet of paper also tends to be easier on the eyes than viewing a tiny screen. Remember the suggestion for keeping track of your billable hours from Chapter 5? A planner is a great place to jot down your time a couple of times a day, along with notes and ideas for projects and cases. Color-coding based on topic or project is also a breeze. You may also want to match this color-coding to the files in your office.

However, regardless of the planner's many benefits, there are drawbacks to consider. First of all, they can be somewhat cumbersome to schlep around from place to place. Even if you choose to use a small one, it's just one more thing you've got to remember to have with you—and small does not always translate into lightweight. Also, smaller ones do not offer the benefit of fitting larger papers securely inside without sticking out and looking sloppy. There's also the issue of privacy because others may gain access to and read or copy sensitive materials. Finally, if you're using it effectively, you will begin to depend on it very heavily, so, if it's ever lost, so are you. Therefore, it is important to consider using some sort of back-up to rely on in a pinch. A few suggestions include scanning addresses and other important information into a document saved in your computer, or duplicating your address book into an electronic organizer.

The Pros and Cons of Using Electronic Organizers

It's not difficult to see why electronic organizers have been so popular, ever since their inception in the early 1990s.[4] They're easy

___

4. According to the ENCYCLOPEDIA BRITANNICA, electronic organizers were once known as "Personal Digital Assistants" (PDAs) and "were devel-

to carry, include various programs and features, and they have the capacity to store more information than many older models of home and office PCs. They're sleek, efficient, and constantly improving. The brick-looking cell phone of the eighties has blossomed into a streamlined mini-computer that's smaller than a pack of cigarettes. They also offer the ability for the user to remain reachable from just about any location. In essence, they enable us to multitask—and to remain cool, calm, and *connected* in the process.

An electronic organizer can hold your address book, access your computer in the office, enable you to read and respond to e-mails, make and receive telephone calls, take pictures, surf the Internet, and even play a few games (assuming you've got the free time). They also enable you to keep information private through either the use of passwords, keeping them turned off when not in use, or due to the difficulty others would have in reading the small screen from a distance. So, what's not to love?

For one thing, electronic devices can be expensive, so they usually require more of a financial investment than planners do. Also, in contrast to planners, whose fees are limited to the purchase price, electronic organizers have associated monthly fees for network access. Since they're constantly improving, they can quickly become obsolete. Much like driving a new car off the lot, the value of an electronic organizer depreciates quickly. It can also take more time to text an entry by using the tiny keys than it would take to pull out a good, old-fashioned pen and pad to write a note. Electronic organizers can also offer unreliable access in some locations, and they can "crash," leaving the user SOL (and I don't mean "School of Law") without a back-up for the information suddenly lost. One idea is to maintain copies of all folders in your home and office computers, replacing the files on a regular basis so that they continue to match as closely as possible. You'll constantly add in-

---

oped ... as digital improvements upon the traditional pen-and-paper organizers used to record personal information[,] such as telephone numbers, addresses, and calendars." *See* www.britannica.com/EBchecked/topic/725975/PDA (accessed March 24, 2015).

formation to the electronic organizer, so it is important to keep re-copying the files for your computer so that you'll lose as little as possible in the event of a malfunction either way. After all, computers crash, too.

Despite their drawbacks, one can only assume that the time saved by having an electronic organizer handy continues to be more valuable than the money spent on their purchase and upkeep. Otherwise, there would only be planners. Instead, both types of personal organizers continue to grow in popularity and available options. The next section will address how to use either—or both—based on your organizational type.

Using Planners and Electronic Organizers by Organizational Type

With the realities of the increased demands on our time as seasoned lawyers and even as beginning law students, it's important to find ways to use planners and electronic organizers to our greatest personal advantage. All organizational types would benefit from using both, but at differing degrees. This translates into using one as your primary source and the other as your secondary source. For those who would prefer to use only one source, you might want to select the "primary" option described for your type. Additionally, for those who insist on only using an electronic organizer, I still recommend having a small notepad and pen to carry at all times.

Stackers and Spreaders may want to use a planner as their primary personal organization tool for a few reasons. First, a planner is a type of stack, which is of natural appeal to Stackers. Stackers may want to invest in extra tabs so that they can create additional stacks within their planners. Spreaders will like the option of being able to add and remove sheets to place with related projects. Additionally, Spreaders would benefit from color-coding so that they can look at their planner and quickly scan the materials based on colors they've associated with clients, cases, and projects. An electronic organizer would then be used solely for making telephone calls, checking e-mails, and keeping primary contact information. Planner contents can be transferred to a separate storage folder to maintain an annual archive.

Free Spirits and Packrats might want to have an electronic organizer as their primary source and also keep a small notepad handy for quick notes. A planner might create too many opportunities to amass haphazard compilations of materials that are a miniature version of their workspaces. In contrast, an electronic organizer is compact, singular, and any messes are invisible. Packrats may want to use a notepad and pen that have personal memories so that they will be more inclined to keep using it. For both types, the notepads can be reviewed regularly to ensure that important items transition to their electronic organizers. When notepads are filled, they can be archived and eventually shredded and tossed. Packrats may want to create a storage box for their used notepads and save the covers and selected pages once the bulk of the contents have been shredded.

Chapter Checklist

✓ Determine whether you are currently using the best combination of planner and electronic organizer for your organizational type.

- Keep expenses in mind when selecting planner styles and electronic organizer formats.
- Select a primary and secondary source based on your organizational type.
- Develop a system for archiving planner contents.

It always seems impossible until it's done.

Nelson Mandela

CHAPTER 7

ORGANIZING
YOUR HOME OFFICE

These days, coming home from a day at the office does not necessarily mean it's time to kick up your feet with the remote. Instead, it's often "part two" of your work day, but in a more relaxed venue. With the high expectations of billable hours, increased (if not unlimited) accessibility (thanks to technology), and the myriad projects constantly competing for first place in line for our attention, many modern lawyers may view the idea of working eight hours a day as an old-fashioned concept from days gone by that doesn't quite mesh with the realities of being a legal professional in the twenty-first century. But just because you must work at home does not mean you cannot do so with style, comfort, and organization.

Unlike your workspace on the job, your home office can be tailored to your personal needs and tastes with greater precision than almost any other environment. It's called *your home office* for a reason, and in that order of importance—it belongs to you, it is located in your home, and it is a place you have designated for work *and* productivity. An increasing number of attorneys either work at home to supplement time spent in the office, or are doing so as solo practitioners.[1] This space may also be visited by clients, vendors, and colleagues. Law students, many of whom also likely work in part-time jobs[2] while in school, typically set up shop at

---

1. For a comprehensive overview, *see* Rebecca Porter, *Balancing Act: Lawyers Working at Home Juggle Job and Family*, TRIAL, February 2001. Although the article was published more than a decade ago, it offers timely advice.

2. Although statistics on law student employment are not widely available, many students may opt to work while in school due to economic ne-

home to study for classes and prepare for final exams. With the demands on our time continuing to increase, maintaining a home office often mirrors the importance of our primary workspace. After all, there are only 24 hours in a day, and if you need to get additional work done, at least at home you can do so in your favorite old pajamas.

However, what is gained in comfort may be sacrificed in efficiency. In contrast to your workspace in the office, it is likely that you are sharing the space designated for your home office with others, which may include a spouse, significant other, children, or roommates. A pet or two might also be in the mix. There could be disruptive noises from neighbors, parties, or traffic. When you're in the office, you can focus on your job with few interruptions because work is the primary focus. However, home is usually a different story. If people and pets are not competing for your time and attention, there are always the television, telephone, and refrigerator calling your name. Therefore, the greatest challenge in creating a home office is setting up a space where you can work the most efficiently with the likelihood that you will be distracted by the least number of, to use torts terminology, attractive nuisances. How do you manage this feat and keep it organized?

This chapter will focus on ideas for creating the best home office for your needs, including suggestions for each organizational type and small ways to personalize your space. Among the topics to be covered include selecting a good working environment, ways to find, use, and repurpose functional furniture, and useful and creative storage ideas.

---

cessity. For a discussion about balancing the concerns of economics and academics while in law school, *see* Shawn P. O'Connor, *How to Decide if You Should Work During Law School*, U.S. NEWS & WORLD REPORT, March 24, 2014.

Selecting a Work Location at Home

Depending on the amount of space you have to work with, a great home office can be as large as the garage or guest bedroom, or as small as a hall closet. For suggestions about workspace measurements, dimensions, and layouts, please see Chapters 2 and 3. The size of your home office is less important than its purpose—and its permanence. Any area you choose to use as your home workspace should be solely used for that purpose for a couple of reasons. The first reason is practical—you need a space where you can store sensitive materials that will not be disturbed, and you also need to have the peace of mind of being able to ascertain that everything will remain as you left it so that you will not waste precious time with reassembly each time you sit down to work. The second reason is psychological—this space needs to be devoted to work and must be seen by you and everyone else in the house as a professional workspace. It cannot be combined with any other home activity. It must be seen as an extension of your office at work, which will serve to lessen the temptation to treat it more as "home" and less as an "office."

There could be a variety of options in your home to choose from, only one obvious choice, or you may need to create an option where none seems to exist. If you have a large home with a few options, select the one that is the quietest and that is the farthest away from the kitchen. Preferably, you may want to choose a room upstairs or one in the basement. If you're living in a small apartment, you can select a section of the living room or bedroom to use as an office, but the challenges there will be to ensure that you treat the space as a workspace. Using a bedroom might be the only option, but the greatest challenge there will be separating work from relaxation. If you must have your home office in the same room where you sleep, it will be very important to keep those activities separate, and also to avoid the temptation to work instead of rest. Converting a closet into a functional workspace is another idea, but this is only an advisable option if you have other places to store clothing (preferably not on the floor). However, one of the benefits of using a closet is the ability to close the door to keep small hands out of your work projects, and it's also a nice way to mentally "close the door" on work and keep it separate from home activities when you're not on the clock, either literally or figuratively.

Just as is true in your workspace in the office, your home office selection will also benefit from considering your organizational type. Stackers and Spreaders might want to choose a spot where there is the possibility of adding open vertical storage. Additionally, Spreaders will need a large surface to spread out the materials they are working on, so any large or small space that they select needs to have room for a table with a large surface. Free Spirits and Packrats may want to choose a location in the house that is not considered a "public" space due to their tendencies to keep and store a lot of extraneous items. If this is not a possibility, another idea would be to select a spot where you can incorporate closed storage—and lots of it. Like the workspace away from home, Free Spirits and Packrats will need to work hard to avoid allowing items to sit around and collect dust—and the challenge to keep up a regular maintenance schedule at home might be greater because this is viewed as a place to relax.

Choosing Home Office Furniture

While your office at work may consist of either a room or a cubicle with a predetermined layout of furnishings beyond your control, your home office is yours to furnish as you wish. Depending on your budget and the amount of space you have to work with, furnishing a home office enables you to infuse your personality into a space. Some people go to office supply stores and purchase replicas of what would be found in a typical corporate environment. If that's your preference, there are plenty of options. Most of the major office supply and furniture stores offer traditional configurations in "L" and "U" shapes in a variety of styles and price ranges. Also, having a home office that has that official "office" look can be helpful for getting in the mood to work or setting a professional tone when working with clients, vendors, and colleagues. Yet another advantage to this style is the potential luxury of designing the "managing partner" office of your dreams away from work that you may not yet have in your current position. Working at home is usually more of a necessity than anything else, but this might be an added incentive to encourage you to mind the chore less and to work harder to keep it organized.

In contrast to recreating a smaller version of the firm environment, you may instead prefer to use eclectic or cozy furniture that focuses more on the "home" part of "home office." This way, you can be creative in your choices of furniture styles, colors, and materials. For example, you may want to shop around at flea markets or estate sales for antique tables, armoires, bookshelves, and chairs. It will also be important to ensure that whatever you choose blends with the décor of the rest of your home.

Instead of purchasing furniture especially for your home office, you might want (or need, due to financial reasons) to repurpose items from other areas of the house. A dining room or game table could serve as an interesting and functional desk, and options for chairs might include using a chair from the dining room and adding an interesting slipcover, plush and sturdy seating from the living room, or even an eclectic outdoor chair brought indoors. Packrats, in particular, may want to use furniture that reminds them of loved ones or other pleasant memories to make their home office special, but this option would appeal to all organizational types.

Regardless of which style you choose, it is important that you select pieces that will serve you well while you are working. The two most important pieces of furniture are a flat surface on which to work and a comfortable chair that offers good support. Stackers and Spreaders may want to look for a desk with one or two drawers. A farm house table is another idea, especially for Spreaders, who will want to have a space to spread their things while they are working. Tables work well for Stackers, provided they are large enough to add vertical storage and other spots to keep stacks within easy reach. Free Spirits and Packrats can use a table, too, provided it offers plenty of space underneath for storage, but they would be better served by instead using a desk with at least two deep drawers. A credenza or an armoire would also be a nice touch to use to store wayward papers and collectibles. Storage will be covered in greater detail in the next section.

Useful and Creative Storage

Often when decorating a workspace, storage is an afterthought. Ironically, this is especially true at home, where attractive storage can have a much greater impact than it would in your workspace in the office. Instead of looking at a bunch of bent, brown moving boxes or a few sad, plastic crates as you're getting your work done, wouldn't it be nicer to use storage that you enjoyed seeing and were proud to display? Not to sound harsh, but if a client were to see where you stored their materials, how would it make them feel about the quality of your representation? Would you be concerned about their opinion? Could this storage withstand damage from the elements, the curiosity of children, or the mischief of pets? If you would feel the need to explain away or apologize for the status of your storage, it's time to make some changes. Fortunately, this is one of the easiest changes you can make.

Storage for your home office need not be expensive to buy or cumbersome to maintain. An added benefit for selecting storage for your home office is the wealth of creative options that are available. In a home office, storage and accessories offer much more flexibility than you have in your workspace at the office. Incorporating functional and creative storage and accessories is one of the least costly ways to personalize your home office — and keep it professional. You may already have the resources you need around the house.

For example, ideas for open storage may include bookshelves, armoires, spice and bakers' racks, and baskets made of wicker, wood, plastic, or cloth. Bins made of metal, plastic, or cloth offer open storage on top, but closed storage on the sides — which can be useful for concealing groupings of items, and can transform storage into something that is both functional and decorative. Faux or real leather boxes are another attractive alternative to brown moving boxes. Look beyond office supply stores for ideas. Containers can be found in home and garden centers, sporting goods stores, and craft shops. Decorative trunks and antique luggage are great options for archiving papers and files. You may also prefer to use file cabinets, but they are typically large, bulky, and can limit the space available for storage options with more personality and pizzazz. Of course, many home offices can effectively include a combination of standard file cabinets and other storage to make the space your own and keep it professional and functional.

Smaller storage options for the surface of your desktop can also be added to suit your style and personal tastes. Household items not originally intended for office use can offer refreshing alternatives to the usual desk sets found in office supply stores. A creamer can hold pens, and a sugar bowl can hold paperclips and other small items that typically float around in a desk drawer. A cigar box could be used to hold chargers for cell phones and other electronic gadgets. Those who may want to add a touch of nostalgia may choose to use a vintage metal lunchbox to store a stapler, tape dispenser, and other tools so that they are instantly transformed from dull necessities to a charming conversation piece. All kinds of small containers can be reused in creative ways. With a little imagination, storage can be economical, functional to use, and a pleasure to see.

Chapter Checklist

✓ Select a space in your home that will solely be used for work.
  • Refer to Chapters 2 and 3 for ideas about measurements, dimensions, and layouts.
  • Choose furniture options that appeal to your personal taste and organizational type. You may want to repurpose household furniture that you already own, or create the "managing partner" office that you do not yet have at work.
  • Regardless of which styles you choose, it is important that you select pieces that will serve you well while you are working. The two most important pieces of furniture are a flat surface on which to work and a comfortable chair that offers good support.
  • Incorporate storage options that are sturdy, functional, creative, and that mesh with your organizational type.

I'm a big believer in the fact that life is about preparation, preparation, preparation.

Johnnie L. Cochran

CHAPTER 8

YOUR PORTABLE OFFICE

In addition to working at home and in the office, sometimes it's necessary to set up shop in other locations. Whether you're working in an alternative space due to travel, hunger, thirst, or the need for a change of scenery, it's important to carry your good organizational habits with you wherever you go. This chapter will focus on the pros and cons of working in a few of the most commonly used alternative work environments. We will also discuss methods to do so while also keeping organized—namely, the importance of creating a portable office.

The most commonly used alternative work locations include airports and airplanes, depots and trains, restaurants, and coffeehouses. Other areas may include libraries, colleagues' offices, conference rooms, and even the great outdoors. There are certainly countless other options (for example, I have heard of business calls taking place in public restrooms, grocery stores, dressing rooms, and in the stands of ball games), but I chose to instead focus on non-transitory places where you might perch for at least an hour at a time on a regular basis with work as your primary focus. Some of them are used by choice, others by necessity. All of them have special considerations that must be kept in mind for legal professionals.[1]

Your Portable Office

If you carried a backpack in law school, you will already understand the concept of a portable office. Having all of your work

---

1. For additional considerations, *see Severing Office "Chains" Calls for Wise Policies*, LAWYER'S PC, August 15, 2013.

tools in one place enables you to work efficiently from just about any location at a moment's notice. Your portable office will be a compact kit that enables you to set up shop and pack it up quickly and efficiently—and to be able to pick up where you left off and know where everything is located.

All organizational types will benefit from having a portable office. Essentially, it consists of a large bag with several compartments that is sturdy enough to tote a laptop, notepad, cell phone, business cards, your planner (discussed in Chapter 6), black, blue, and red pens, two colors of highlighters, a pencil with an eraser, earplugs, post-it notes, tissues, hand sanitizer, a back-up battery (if necessary), and a charger. If you wear glasses or take medication, you may also want to include a small bag for essential toiletries, and you might want to include a daily dosage that's always there, just in case.

There are many attractive options of bags to use, including tote bags, satchels, and large laptop carriers. Possible selections can be made of leather or cloth, but any bag you choose for this purpose should look professional and polished because you will be carrying it everywhere and it needs to represent you as the capable professional that you are. This is one item that will need to be able to withstand use and abuse with grace and style, so you may want to splurge on a piece that will only improve with age.

Your portable office is designed to be the foundation that enables you to move from place to place to work on just about any project. It is not designed to replace your home and work offices. You may want to bring one project with you at a time and devote one large section of the bag to any materials you need for that particular task. After each use of your portable office, unpack the contents of the project you were working on and keep the foundational contents intact for the bag's next use. Check to see if any restocking of supplies is necessary after each use. It can be frustrating to assume that you have what you need and find that it is not there when you need it.

Airports and Airplanes

The most positive aspect of working in an airport or airplane is the knowledge that you are putting travel time to productive use. You can get a lot done on a laptop or by reading files either online or in a small stack of papers. Looking and actually being busy are also great ways to deflect unwanted attention from chatty seatmates. The downsides of working in airports and airplanes include tight spaces, loud noises, constant interruptions, and crowded conditions. With people practically sitting in your lap, you must be especially careful not to permit curious eyes from seeing confidential materials.

Although the cons may seem to outweigh the pros, many attorneys spend enough time traveling to necessitate the effort to work in these locations. To do so most effectively, you may want to use a very streamlined portable office, make sure your bag meets the measurement requirements for air travel, and be sure to include earplugs or an electronic device that will enable you to listen to music to drown out excessive noise. If it's within your budget, you may also want to invest in a smaller device that will be easier to maneuver on the tray associated with your seat.

Depots and Trains

If you have a long commute to the office or are traveling by rail on a longer trip, you may want to use the time to get some work done. While many of the pros and cons of working in depots and trains mirror those of air travel, another element to consider is the repeated stops and starts and how that might impact your ability to keep everything on your lap.

Although some people use their cell phones on trains, doing so could make it difficult to maintain confidentiality. Plus, no one else likes hearing someone else's conversations in these conditions; it can be somewhat rude and disruptive. If you must make or take a call, keep it brief and general so as not to disturb other passengers. I realize we're all busy, but lengthy calls can usually wait until you've reached your destination. If a demanding colleague, partner, or client is on the line and insists on talking right then and there, your options for ending the call may be limited, and it may be challenging to concentrate. If this happens, try to jot down some notes as soon as you reach your destination so that you can have a record that might be useful at a later date.

Restaurants and Coffeehouses

The best thing these two locations have going for them is access to unlimited fresh coffee and beverages, as well as a variety of meals and snacks. However, this availability can become distracting if you are taking more coffee breaks than getting work done. Coffeehouses also offer the added benefit of being open early and closed late, and some restaurants are open 24 hours a day. Some people are drawn to these options for the change of scenery and decreased distractions from adults, children, and pets at home. Many coffeehouses offer wireless connections.

However, distractions can come from the loud music that coffeehouse often play or from the conversations from neighboring tables. You may be required to purchase items to keep your table, and you must be careful not to spill anything on important documents. Also, the tables tend to be small and arranged so that they are close together, which makes it difficult to spread out materials as you work and necessitates making an effort to make sure confidential information stays that way.

Chapter Checklist

✓ Create a portable office that you can carry, reuse, pack, and unpack, and that can be used in a variety of locations at a moment's notice. This benefits all organizational types.

- Always carry business cards when working offsite. You never know what kinds of contacts might develop.
- Consider the pros and cons of working in public spaces before actually doing so.
- Maintain a heightened awareness of the potential challenges of preserving client confidentiality in public locations.
- Try to adjust to tight spaces and other inconveniences that may not exist in your permanent workspaces at home and in the office.
- Enjoy the benefits of using your time wisely and maintaining high levels of productivity away from your home and office workspaces.

A love of books, of holding a book, turning its pages, looking at its pictures, and living its fascinating stories goes hand-in-hand with a love of learning.

Laura Bush

Chapter 9

Home and Office Libraries

Having a library in your home and office workspaces is not as lofty as it sounds, and having a few references on hand can save you valuable time as you're working on projects. Although many of the following titles have online access, it will be important to be prepared for times when systems are down or you do not have access to a computer. Also, much like our discussion of the differences between using a planner versus an electronic organizer, sometimes it's faster and more efficient to flip through a few pages in a book instead of scrolling through screens on a computer.

During law school and in practice, attorneys typically spend a lot of time doing research online, in books, or both. Although the Internet offers a wealth of information in subscription and free databases, there are some resources in print that should always have a place in an attorney's office. We all remember from law school that books are often expensive, and many can quickly become obsolete as new editions are introduced to take the place of older ones. For that reason, and in consideration of the space you have to work with, you may want to limit your collection to the following reference materials, as well as to books that are especially suited to your practice area(s). You can then supplement your permanent collection with materials found online and in firm or public law libraries.

Essentially, a library is a collection of books that are amassed for personal or professional interests. The collection needn't be large or expensive to be useful and of great professional value. A good library can be as small as one shelf or it can fill up a series of rooms. Although you may have a lot of space to devote to libraries at home and work, this chapter will address basic contents from which you can build over time. These materials can fit on a shelf in a bookcase, or, if you're pressed for space, they can be stored in a large basket and labeled for easy access. This entire list should cost less than $1,000, and it requires infrequent updates.

Recommended Reference Materials

Whether you could win a spelling bee without preparation, or have trouble spelling "misspell," it is important to have good legal and general dictionaries and thesauri. Of course, *Black's Law Dictionary*[1] remains a top source for legal dictionaries, and those of the general variety include *Webster's*[2] and the *Oxford English Dictionary*.[3] Although dictionaries include synonyms and antonyms as part of definitions, it is important to have legal and general thesauri for additional word choice ideas. One of the most commonly used legal thesauri is *Burton's*,[4] and *Roget's*[5] is a good one of the general variety.

There are many legal reference materials available, but two of the most useful ones are *The Bluebook*[6] and *The Redbook*.[7] Yet another is the *Bieber Dictionary of Legal Abbreviations*.[8] Many recent

---

1. BLACK'S LAW DICTIONARY, 10th ed., Bryan A. Garner, Editor (Thomson West, 2014).

2. THE MERRIAM-WEBSTER DICTIONARY, 11th ed. (Merriam-Webster, Inc., 2004).

3. CONSISE OXFORD ENGLISH DICTIONARY, 12th ed. (Oxford University Press, 2011).

4. BURTON'S LEGAL THESAURUS, 5th ed., by William C. Burton (McGraw-Hill, 2013).

5. THE CONCISE ROGET'S INTERNATIONAL THESAURUS, 7th ed. , by Barbara Ann Kipfer (HarperCollins, 2011).

6. THE BLUEBOOK: A UNIFORM SYSTEM OF CITATION, 20th ed. (Harvard Law Review Association, 2015).

7. THE REDBOOK: A MANUAL ON LEGAL STYLE, 3rd ed., by Bryan A. Garner (West, 2013).

8. PRINCE'S BIEBER DICTIONARY OF LEGAL ABBREVIATIONS, 6th ed., by Mary Miles Prince (Hein, 2009).

law school graduates may have used the *ALWD Manual*[9] instead of *The Bluebook*, but the latter is commonly used for citations in law review articles and court opinions; for this reason, if you do not have a copy, it's worth the modest investment.[10]

As for general reference materials, an etiquette guide[11] is essential and is not typically found in every law library. This is an important and handy reference that can guide you through a variety of potential uncertainties, such as how to address same-sex couples in letters, the use of official titles, formats for correspondence, and diagrams of various table settings. If you need to brush up on the rules of writing, two classic guides are *The Elements of Style*[12] and *The Chicago Manual of Style*.[13] *The Redbook*, as mentioned previously, is another solid resource. To complete the collection, a current local telephone book and a world atlas can literally help you get from points A to B. Although many people rely on the Web for telephone numbers and directions, remember that some clients may still prefer to let their fingers do the walking; additionally, these print resources can be quite useful as a back-up, or for the vision impaired.

Library Organization

Although libraries consist of books, it is somewhat ironic that bookshelves tend to look better when they're not stuffed with ma-

---

9. ALWD Guide to Legal Citation, 5th ed., by the Association of Legal Writing Directors and Coleen M. Barger (Wolters Kluwer, 2014).

10. For another useful list of print and electronic resources, *see* Mary Whisner, *Books on My Desk*, Law Library Journal, Fall 2012.

11. Emily Post's The Etiquette Advantage in Business, Third Edition: Personal Skills for Professional Success, by Peter Post, with Anna Post, Lizzie Post, and Daniel Post Senning (William Morrow, 2014); Global Business Etiquette: A Guide to International Communication and Customs, by Jeanette S. Martin and Lillian H. Chaney (Praeger, 2012).

12. The Elements of Style, 4th ed., by William Strunk and E.B. White (Longman, 1999).

13. The Chicago Manual of Style, 16th ed. (University of Chicago Press, 2010).

terials. Just as you have weeded through papers and files when organizing your home and office workspaces, you will also need to do the same with books and other contents in your library. (For a detailed discussion of weeding and sorting, please see Chapter 1.) Some items may need to be tossed or archived so that you will have room for what you need to keep—but without the clutter of materials that are not immediately useful. You may decide to retain some books in your collection for sentimental reasons, but it is better to do so at home than at work. A few quirky additions in your office on the job are welcome and help to show a little personality, but having more than 25 percent of your collection devoted to nonessential titles is a luxury that few can afford to maintain without the space becoming cluttered, unkempt, and unfocused.

Once you've weeded and archived and are left with the books that you will keep, you may want to "catalog" them by topic, arranging them in sections based on practice materials, legal reference, and periodicals. To save space, one idea is to subscribe to newspapers and magazines online and to only print articles that you need to keep. For magazines that you must retain in print, invest in inexpensive magazine holders and group them by title. Typically, one magazine holder can hold a year of issues, and it looks much more polished than leaving them stacked or scattered on the floor. Unless magazines and periodicals are essential for your areas of practice and cannot be conveniently accessed in other libraries, you may need to consider limiting the number of issues on hand in your office to one year's worth per title and archiving the rest. Once you've decided where everything will be stored both inside and outside of your workspaces at home and in the office, you may also want to create a list of all of the titles available and place this sheet in the "Reference" folder on your desk (assuming you have adopted the System, which was discussed in Chapter 3).

Organizational Types and Library Design

Each organizational type will have different strengths and weaknesses with building and maintaining home and office libraries. Stackers and Spreaders will tend to arrange their bookshelves in neat piles, but Stackers will need to be careful not to allow piles to accumulate. Spreaders will need to remember to close books and shelve them—especially if they're in the midst of a project. Otherwise, they will return to a workspace that has papers spread out with one or two books among the papers to weed through to start anew. Free Spirits will do an effective job of compiling materials related to their areas of practice and that appeal to their personal interests, but they will face a constant struggle with getting rid of items that seem too interesting to part with. Thus, they will need to develop a regular weeding schedule that they will realistically stick with. Packrats will need to make sure they keep their shelves available for books without permitting cherished memorabilia to encroach on the space. Like Free Spirits, Packrats will need to develop a regular weeding schedule. Both Free Spirits and Packrats would also benefit from adding closed storage elements to their libraries in order to group and conceal materials.

Chapter Checklist

✓ Consider investing in several basic reference materials, including: legal and non-legal dictionaries and thesauri; sources for legal abbreviations and citations; a business etiquette guide; writing style manuals; a local telephone book; and a world atlas.

   • Just as you have weeded through papers and files when organizing your home and office workspaces, you will also need to do the same with books and other contents in your home and office libraries.

   • Once you've weeded and archived and are left with the books that you will keep, you may want to "catalog" them by topic, arranging them in sections based on practice materials, legal reference, and periodicals.

   • Create a list of available titles and store it in the "Reference" file on your desk.

   • Develop a weeding schedule that you will realistically stick with.

   • Visit public or law firm libraries for ideas about space design and book placement.

Marketing is far too important to leave to the marketing department.

David Packard

Chapter 10

Marketing and Social Media

Some like to call it marketing or public relations. Others refer to it as client development or networking. No matter what you call it, it will involve entertaining, social media, and keeping in touch. Maintaining solid relationships with clients and cultivating new ones must be part of what attorneys do on a regular basis. Entertaining is one of the best ways to socialize in a productive way, and using social media wisely is a useful way to consistently enhance and support the relationships that have been cultivated over time.

Many attorneys balk at the notion of marketing for fear that they will appear sleazy. Instead, they insist that their good work will speak for itself, which will lead to a strong client base. Although good work is crucial, so is networking. Meeting people and solidifying relationships is an unspoken part of what it means to be an effective lawyer. Granted, it is important to respect the directives in the Rules of Professional Conduct as they relate to advertising, but it is possible to entertain in a way that is polished and professional without being stuffy and uncomfortable. Developing relationships and getting to know new and existing clients better through entertaining can have far-reaching effects on your future as a legal professional. In contrast to offensive images of ambulance chasers and used car salesmen, entertaining is more of a public relations activity because it is not openly selling your services, but is instead gently letting people get to know you and what you can do to professionally assist them, with a pleasant activity as an attractive diversion.

Most large law firms have in-house marketing departments that plan events and seminars and handle the creation of brochures, newsletters, and other publications.[1] Smaller firms and solo practitioners may not have marketing staffs, but they must still consider ways to reach current clients and develop new business. Attorneys working in corporate or government settings must often socialize with other departments within their work environments, which are typically akin to external clients. Entertaining is an expectation for lawyers working in all types of settings.

In journalism, a good story answers the questions of who, what, where, when, why, and how. The same is true for successful event planning. This chapter will focus on each of these elements, which should be considered when planning and attending events, along with a brief overview of various social media platforms that are most frequently used by lawyers in a professional capacity. You may have event planners, office staff, or colleagues who will take care of event logistics, but your job as a host or a guest will be much easier and more fruitful if you approach these occasions in an organized fashion. You may be asked for suggestions or feedback, so considering these questions and keeping information handy will serve you well as you maneuver through the socializing process. The more you know, the more comfortable you are, and the more fun you can have.

Who?

The most important element of entertaining clients or anyone else involves the guest list. Who will attend your event? Are there certain clients you would like to have in attendance? Are there others you would like to attract? Would you like to have media coverage, or is this going to be more of a private affair? The number of people attending and their particular interests will guide every-

---

1. According to a recent survey, only 20 percent of law firms use social networking or alumni programs to attract and retain clients. *See* LAW OFFICE MANAGEMENT & ADMINISTRATION REPORT, Institute of Management & Administration, July 2008. *See also* Maria Kantza Velos, *Law Firm Marketing is More Than Skin Deep*, CHICAGO LAWYER, June 2008.

thing else that you may decide to include in the event. For this reason, you may want to keep track of the interests and hobbies your
clients and colleagues have so that you can refer to them as you
plan events and create guest lists. On the backs of business cards
or in a database that you may decide to create in a Excel spreadsheet, jot down favorite teams, restaurants, music, or films that
you have discussed in passing so that you can refer to these interests as you decide whom to invite to which events. Creating a
spreadsheet offers the added benefit of being able to sort the names
by fields. For example, if you wanted to host an event during a
baseball game, you could consult the spreadsheet and sort it with
the keyword of "baseball" to determine which clients and colleagues would most enjoy this activity.

What?

What types of activities will you offer? In contrast to seminars
where you might showcase your legal expertise, entertaining involves
cultivating relationships in a more personal way that is still professional. Unlike the old days when the legal profession was more of
an "old boy's" club, these days attorneys and clients are much more
diverse, and so are their interests. As a result, not everyone enjoys
sporting events, 18 holes of golf, or a thick, juicy Rib Eye. Many still
do, but a little creativity could lead to events that are less standard
and more unforgettable.

A great way to develop ideas is to visit the web pages of other
law firms to see what types of events they have hosted. Ask colleagues who work in other firms. You may also see events covered
in the "Society" section of some newspapers, as well as the "On the
Scene" section in local magazines. Creativity need not be expensive to be memorable and appreciated. No one wants to attend yet
another chicken dinner with a speaker whose remarks are forgot-
ten before they've begun. If you hear about a great idea for an
event, add it to your database, or send yourself an e-mail to file
away in an "Event Ideas" folder online.

When?

Attorneys are not the only ones who are extremely busy. Clients, too, have tight schedules that fill up quickly, especially when they are in the upper echelons of a company and are expected to attend myriad functions around the clock. What time of day will work best for the majority of invited guests? How much advance notice must be provided for invitations? Will you send "Save the Date" cards or e-mails? Many busy attorneys group entertaining with meals for the sake of efficiency, preferring breakfast or lunch meetings to dinner events in order to preserve as much time as possible for work-life balance.

Some types of activities, such as sporting events or theatrical performances, will dictate the time of your events; however, if you are planning an outing that will last at least two hours, you would be better served doing so in a way that permits conversation and allows guests to discreetly come and go without feeling trapped. If you're trying to narrow down possible dates, there are companies in several cities that offer social calendars that provide information about the major events of the year so that you will be less inclined to schedule an event that conflicts with your guests' schedules.

Most importantly, you need to check your own calendar and determine when you can realistically take the time to do extensive entertaining and also commit to regularly-scheduled activities. Even though entertaining takes time away from work, it is as much a part of your position as attending meetings in the office. As a result, try to attend or plan a work-related entertainment activity once a week, and budget your time accordingly. You might even physically block out the time in your calendar.

Where?

Depending on where you live and work, you may have countless possible locations or only a few possible settings to work with in planning an event. There are different considerations based on venues, which may include the office, your home, or another location. Create a database to record details for each large event you attend, or send yourself e-mails and file them away to refer to for future events.

Entertaining colleagues and clients in your home should be done on a limited scale, and only for those whom you know well or intend to foster long-lasting relationships. Cooking and socializing at the same time can be a chore, so you might consider hiring a caterer. Many larger firms have a variety of sizes and styles of rooms in which to entertain, as do many corporate offices. However, some clients may appreciate attending functions at a venue that is more eclectic or suited to the occasion. Examples of creative options that retain a professional air include art galleries, museum lobbies, and stately older mansions that are rented out for parties. Hotels are often dull, unless they are located in luxury vacation spots. An inexpensive way to locate ideas is to contact the local Convention and Visitor's Bureau in your area to request a welcome packet. It will include contact information for a variety of venues that you may not have been aware of—even if you have lived in the area for years.

Why?

What is the purpose of this event? Socializing is the primary reason, but you may also want to host or attend an event to interact with several people at once who don't often have schedules that mesh, or you may want to attract new clients. Is the activity tailored to the interests of your guests? Have you set goals of numbers of people you will meet and with whom you will mingle?

How?

How did it go? Feedback is important, and it can be garnered formally or informally. Also, consider having a meeting with colleagues to discuss the pros and cons of the event, and whether it met your goals. For large-scale events, consider sending a survey to guests, particularly for annual meetings, conferences, and CLE courses.

Additional Considerations

You will need to remember to have and hand out business cards. For cards you receive, write the date and event on the backs of each card to remind you of how and where you met each guest, and store cards in a business card file. Consider sending thank-you notes by postal mail to all guests. If you are a guest yourself, make sure you have nice note cards to write a quick note by hand. Avoid sending "thank you" e-mails because they do not help you to stand out. Even though an electronic message of gratitude is somewhat thoughtful, it can never replace the positive reputation that comes from the time and care of doing so the old-fashioned way. Moreover, an e-mail is much easier to delete. For those who are trying to be environmentally friendly, consider using note cards made of recycled paper.

For additional details about the intricacies of entertaining, you may want to purchase and consult an etiquette guide; suggested titles may be found in Chapter 9. Ensure that any gifts comply with your clients' company gift policies. Think about dietary restrictions, and keep those on file in a database with each guest.

Social Media—An Organized Approach

There are myriad articles outlining the "dos and don'ts" of effective social media usage for lawyers.[2] This section will discuss tips for using social media for professional purposes in an organized way. This essentially involves keeping track of what was said, when

---

2. *See, e.g.,* Mary Kate Sheridan, *Social Media Gone Wrong,* LEGAL MANAGEMENT, June 2012; Kelly Lynn Anders, *Ethical Exits: When Lawyers and Judges Must Sever Ties on Social Media,* CHARLESTON LAW REVIEW, Vol. 7, No. 2, Winter 2012–2013.

it was said, and to whom. Keeping track of social media messaging is especially important because it ensures that you have a handle on "managing your messaging"—which leads to maintaining control over an important aspect of your professional identity.

As of 2015, the most commonly used social media platforms for professional purposes are LinkedIn and Twitter. Both are well suited to a lawyer's needs because they are primarily text driven and provide opportunities to post brief, informative snippets and links to news, newsletters, and topics that relate to one's areas of practice. How do organizational considerations mesh with social media?

As an example, a tax lawyer may wish to post an item about an article that he or she has authored, a CLE presentation, or a link to a news item that would be useful to his or her clients. A recommended way to keep track of postings and subject matter would be to develop a thematic editorial calendar of topics that will be addressed on a monthly, quarterly, or annual basis, thereby providing more focus to the content of messaging, as well as a reference tool to consult to see what was previously posted—which eliminates (or significantly reduces) the likelihood of redundancy.

Yet another consideration is to save time via cross platform postings—but to do so wisely. Many programs will enable a posting on one platform to automatically post on another. As an example, one can simultaneously post on Facebook and Twitter. However, taking advantage of this option can easily lead to a poorer quality of postings on the secondary source, particularly in instances where a Facebook posting is longer than the 140 characters allowed on Twitter; in those instances, the full Facebook posting will be shortened on Twitter, with a link to the original Facebook posting. This is counterproductive to the original sense of efficiency of using the cross-platform posting feature because not all viewers will take the time to click the link to see the full text of the original post. Furthermore, if the tweet provides a link back to the Facebook page, this could be problematic in some workplaces because there are many employers that do not permit access to Facebook on company time. Therefore, before setting up the cross-posting option, it is important to consider how the postings will look on all platforms, and it is especially important to ensure that you're using social media methods that can be viewed in professional environments.

Chapter Checklist

✓ Developing relationships and getting to know new and existing clients better through entertaining can have far-reaching effects on your future as a legal professional.
  - Consider the "who, what, when, where, why, and how" of planning a successful event.
  - Be thoughtful and creative in entertaining clients, which will encourage them to consider you and your firm to be memorable in positive ways.
  - Create a database with colleagues' and clients' interests and dietary restrictions.
  - Avoid electronic "thank you" cards. Send nice ones via postal mail instead.
  - Invest in an etiquette guide to guide you through the intricacies of entertaining. Large law firms may also have marketing staffs that can assist with the nuts and bolts of planning successful events.
  - Consider using a brief survey for large-scale events, particularly those with a CLE component.

I don't mind making jokes, but I don't want to look like one.

Marilyn Monroe

CHAPTER 11

LOOKING THE PART

Being an organized lawyer extends to your appearance. Whether you're meeting with clients, or sequestered in your office working on a brief, it's crucial that you look the part of an attorney who is polished, professional, and in control. It is possible to achieve this look without spending thousands of dollars, enduring discomfort, or expending a lot of effort. Additionally, it is something that any attorney can accomplish, regardless of age, gender, nationality, or clothing size. All it takes is a little time, a modest budget, and a lot of honesty. Whether you look like you've stepped out of a magazine or are a walking fashion *faux pas*, there's always room for improvement.

Seasoned lawyers may recall the days when attorneys were expected to wear suits and ties—even on days when they were not scheduled to meet with clients. Younger lawyers, in contrast, may see this as stiff and unnecessary, instead opting for a more casual look when they're not meeting with clients or making court appearances. Some might say that they are going too far.[1] However, these practices are not always associated with age. There are many senior lawyers who err on the side of being too casual and younger lawyers who prefer the Brooks Brothers look. Like other professions, the legal profession seems to be at a crossroads in what professional attire should look like and how it should be defined.[2]

---

1. *See* Christina Binkley, *Law Without Suits: New Hires Flout Tradition*, THE WALL STREET JOURNAL, January 31, 2008. *But see* Pressly M. Millen, *I Like My Professional Uniform*, THE NATIONAL LAW JOURNAL, April 21, 2008 (discussing the importance of traditional attire).

2. *See* Harold M. Goldner, *You're Going to Wear That? Appearance in the Workplace*, GPSOLO, January/February 2010 (discussing the establishment of dress codes).

Unfortunately, like a lot of case law, there are few clear-cut answers. There are many "dress for success" books on the market, but none specifically addresses the needs of lawyers. Some work environments may provide guidance in this area, but most do not. Many law school career services offices offer various levels of guidance for students who are interviewing for jobs, but the topic is not typically part of the traditional law school curriculum.[3] As a result, there are many well-educated professionals who do not know how to "look the part" and employers who do not know the best way to gingerly approach them without being offensive.

This chapter will include suggestions for what to wear and avoid wearing at various functions that lawyers are typically required or expected to attend, staples that belong in every lawyer's wardrobe, seasonal considerations, shopping lists for men and women, and a few suggestions for ways to keep your wardrobe organized. We will begin with what has become one of the most challenging questions faced by attorneys of all ages who are working in all areas of practice—how to handle "business casual" in a legal environment.

"Business Casual" for Lawyers

The term, "business casual," is a prime example of opposites being combined into an unclear concept that was ironically developed to make things easier. We all know what "business" attire means, and "casual" is clear, but together they tend to cause a lot of confusion. Where does "business" end and "casual" begin, or vice versa? How dressy is "business" and how unstructured is "casual" in this equation? How does a lawyer pull off this look in a way that puts colleagues and clients at ease?

Essentially, "business casual" literally puts business first and casual second. It is a look that is polished, but easygoing and sim-

---

3. *See, e.g.,* Erik M. Jensen, *Law School Attire: A Call for a Uniform Uniform Code,* OKLAHOMA CITY UNIVERSITY LAW REVIEW, 2007; *see also* Piper Fogg, *Frump & Circumstance,* THE CHRONICLE OF HIGHER EDUCATION, September 14, 2007.

ple. It combines business and casual attire in a way that is still professional enough to convey an air of authority. As a general rule, if you could wear something to work out, play sports, do yard work, or build sandcastles, it crosses into the casual zone and is not polished enough for a business setting. Conversely, wearing a tailored suit and wingtips with a golf shirt is neither business, nor casual—it's just confused. However, pairing a suit with a collared shirt, no tie, and oxfords could qualify as business casual. It's an issue of balance without going to either extreme.

As for collared shirts, business casual for men can include those of the colorful, buttoned-down variety, as long as they are in a traditional style. This look works especially well with a blazer and khaki trousers. Women can wear blouses with lively prints, provided that they fit well and do not show too much cleavage. Business casual attire also means that men needn't wear ties and women can avoid pantyhose and still achieve the look.

It is even possible to maintain a crisp, professional look while wearing a t-shirt and sandals—provided that you choose wisely. For example, most t-shirts with words are too casual to wear in the office. The exception is a shirt that has a company or firm logo on it, but that is also crisp and professional. The most common type of acceptable company or firm shirt to wear to work is a collared golf shirt with a small logo placed on the top left or right corner. But even this option must be exercised with caution. Displaying loyalty is important, but looking like a daily advertisement may come across as excessive, insincere, or just plain unimaginative. People will start to wonder how and why you have accumulated so much company-inspired merchandise.

Plain t-shirts work best. They can be crisp white or in classic colors, in crew and v-neck styles, and with or without a pocket. Ideally, they should be made of natural fibers, such as silk or cotton. Cotton t-shirts are the most economical, and they are washable and inexpensive to replace. Silk tees, in contrast, typically require dry cleaning. Some cotton tees include a hint of Lycra, which can enhance a good fit. Speaking of fit, avoid tees that are either too loose or too tight. The best way to ascertain a good fit is to make sure the tee gently touches the body with no more than an inch of extra fabric on each side of your torso, the arms are not too tight, and the shirt is long enough to tuck in, if necessary, but also short enough to wear outside of your skirt or trousers without going past the middle of your rear end. Finally, when white t-shirts start to lose their sparkle or colored tees begin to fade, stop wearing them into the office and buy replacements. If you're unsure about how bright your white tees really are, compare them to a sheet of paper.

As for open-toed shoes, men and women have a variety of options, but leather sandals are the best choice. Also, make sure your feet and toenails are well-groomed before wearing open-toed shoes into the office. Although there are very nice "flip flop" sandals available for men and women, it can be very challenging to pull off this look while still looking and feeling professional. A good rule of thumb is to avoid wearing any open-toed shoes to the office that you would not worry about ruining while walking in mud or sand. If they can be cared for with a hose instead of with shoe polish, they probably will not provide the professional polish you need as a legal professional. As a caveat, there are also many closed-toed, expensive shoes that are made of fine materials, but are simply not professional. Examples include Uggs, hiking boots, Doc Martens, and any type of shoe that you must wear to play sports. It's great if you like Mike, but leave the Nikes and other athletic attire at home. This includes jerseys and baseball caps.

To sum up, clothing that qualifies as business casual is tailored like business attire, but borrows casual elements from the use of easy, washable fabrics. Khaki trousers are an example of this principle, as are well-fitting (which does not mean snug or tight) cotton skirts and dresses, and even tailored denim jeans and blazers (although denim is still forbidden in some workplaces). The key is to select items that are cut like business attire, but are made of fabrics that are less fussy and formal. It's a step up from casual, but it's still all business. For general ideas on what qualifies, please refer to the shopping lists later in this chapter.

What to Wear to "Lawyer" Functions

Attorneys attend all types of events—too many to list in this chapter. This section will address attire considerations for some of the most common events that lawyers are expected to attend. We will also discuss questions to consider when you're making decisions of what to wear to any professional event. Although general daily work attire will not be covered in this section, the shopping lists and wardrobe staples that appear later in this chapter will provide guidance in that area.

The most common types of functions include receptions, barbeques, cocktail parties, formal dinners, law school alumni events, and firm retreats. Most events involve refreshments, a social element, and often a speaker. In determining what to wear, it may help to borrow from the "who, what, where, when, why, and how" questions posed in Chapter 10, but with a slightly different twist. *Who will be there?* In other words, will this event involve clients, colleagues, or neither? If possible, you may want to see whether you can obtain a copy of the guest list beforehand so that you know who will be there and can prepare accordingly. *What will be happening?* The tone of the event will guide your clothing selections, as will the attire advisory on the invitation. *When will the event take place?* Typically, events that are scheduled during the evening tend to be more formal than those that occur during the day. *Where will it be held?* Will it involve getting out in the elements or a long walk? These are considerations to keep in mind for your selections of clothing and shoes. *Why are you attending?* If you're going to be there in an official capacity, it may mean that you may be asked to provide brief, impromptu remarks, which means that you may want to wear something that makes you feel especially confident. *How do you want to be perceived?* You may want to wear something that helps you blend in with the crowd, or you may instead prefer to stand out in a positive way.

For any lawyer-type event that you must attend, it is important that you are perceived as a professional. This does not mean that you should show up to a barbeque or a retreat in a suit and tie. Instead, it means that any clothing you wear in an official capacity should reflect you as polished, professional, and appropriately dressed for the occasion. So, if we were to select clothing for the events mentioned above, men may choose to wear a nice suit and tie to receptions, cocktail parties, and law school alumni events, and women could select a dress or a nice suit. Khaki trousers and a crisp shirt would be the men's selection for more casual occasions, such as retreats and barbeques. Women have a bit more flexibility because they could choose to wear a nice skirt or dress instead of slacks.

Although barbeques are by far the most casual event listed, wearing jeans would only be appropriate if you knew everyone well and knew that others would be wearing them, and even then they would need to be nice jeans that don't have the "I've had these for 10 years" look. For women who choose to wear jeans, avoid the "low rise" style so that you can be seated without showing your seat. Additionally, please note that some workplaces still do not permit jeans; in these cases, khaki and corduroy trousers are a polished alternative. As for skirts, it is possible to keep them feminine and flattering without wearing them too tight or going too far above the knee. Ideally, professional skirts should fall no higher than two inches above the knee in order to avoid showing your ... *briefs.*

Wardrobe Staples

There are several items that belong in every lawyer's closet. If you are trying to build your professional wardrobe on a budget, these are pieces that you can collect over time. If possible, try to purchase the highest quality of each of these items that you can afford. That way, they will last a long time—and they will always serve you well. Please also remember that it is not necessary or advisable to select items that are flashy or ostentatious. Instead, keep them understated so that they will blend with other elements, while also standing the test of time with style, grace, and flair. The idea is to look effortlessly stylish, not like you are trying too hard.

A Few Good Suits—Great suits need not cost thousands of dollars apiece to be well made and look good on you. The most important things to remember are to choose suits that have a cut that flatters you, are made with a good quality fabric, include lining, and are in colors of muted or classic tones that can be worn repeatedly without looking dated. Classic styles are best because they are less likely to go out of style and they are always appropriate. You may need to have your suits tailored to ensure a proper fit. Some department stores offer tailoring services along with your purchase for a modest additional fee.

A Few Pairs of Leather Shoes—There's nothing that makes a day longer than wearing uncomfortable shoes. They hurt to walk in, and every step is a chore. Men may want to have a few pairs of shoes in various styles in black and brown leather. Women might want to look for stylish flats and pumps in black, brown, and navy. You can add other styles and colors once you've covered the basics. Most importantly, make sure these shoes fit like gloves. Splurge, if necessary. Beautiful and comfortable shoes can make all the difference with any outfit.

A Stylish Blazer or Sport Coat—This is separate from a suit jacket, but has a similar shape. A great blazer or sport coat can be worn in business and business casual settings, and is usually made of a textured, but understated, fabric. Like your suits, make sure this jacket fits you well.

A Nice Watch—The best thing about a nice watch is that it can be the epitome of style and substance because it looks nice and tells time. It also looks much more professional than pulling out your cell phone to see what time it is. Selecting the right one for you also enables you to literally display a little personality, which can turn your timepiece into a conversation piece. Packrats, in particular, may want to wear a watch that is a gift from a loved one, but this option would appeal to any organizational type. Younger lawyers may want to avoid pocket watches, or any other timepiece that appears too slick or stylized.

A Leather Briefcase or Satchel—A leather bag that can hold everything you need for your portable office (which was discussed in Chapter 8) will enhance your professional look. These bags are typically expensive, usually $300 to $500 minimum. However, once you make the initial investment, these bags tend to improve with age, and they look so much more polished than a duffel bag or a backpack.

A Good Coat and Trench Coat—The right outerwear enhances the rest of your ensemble and demonstrates excellent attention to detail. Nothing ruins a great outfit more than a coat that is either in ill repair or does not mesh with formal or business attire; an example is pairing a casual ski jacket over a business suit. A lined, wool coat in black or brown and a khaki or black trench coat will last for years and match everything. You may want to look for a trench coat with a removable lining so that it can be worn year-round. Since these items also tend to be expensive, you may want to purchase them during off-season sales or in warmer climates. I bought two of my nicest, warmest coats in Southern California nearly 20 years ago, and they still elicit compliments whenever I wear them. You may not think people notice, but they do.

Seasonal Considerations

In addition to having proper outerwear to blend with your clothing, it is also a good idea to select articles of clothing that can be worn in multiple seasons. Timeless and "seasonless" pieces will help you build and maintain your professional wardrobe with efficiency, and you can also add a few seasonal items each year to keep your look fresh and current. The easiest and least expensive way to add seasonal items is through accessories. For example, women can add an assortment of summer and winter scarves, while men may decide to wear ties in lighter colors during the warmer months.

Another way to change your look each season is with shoes and shirts. You might want to check with your firm or company to see whether there are any policies in place against open-toed shoes before investing in them too heavily. Additionally, you might also want to check to see if there are similar policies in place with your clients' places of business so that you can continue to blend in when you must visit their offices for meetings. Women should also verify that they may wear open-toed shoes while in court. Men are advised to avoid short-sleeved, button-down shirts during any time of year. A long-sleeved shirt with the sleeves rolled up looks much more upscale and pulled together—even during the hot, summer months.

A Note on Tattoos

If you have tattoos or piercings, wear shirts that conceal them. This may sound archaic, but the law is still a field that is mired in tradition, and, in many firms, tattoos are still taboo.[4] Although it may be considered body art to you and you have a right to express yourself in your own time, the look is still not considered professional by many employers and it may be a turn-off to some clients.[5]

Shopping Lists for Men and Women

Every work environment is different, and trends can vary by region, so the following lists are intended to serve as a general guide of all of the types of clothing that you might need for professional occasions. Items that are *italicized* were also discussed in the section of this chapter that focused on "Wardrobe Staples," but I have

---

4. For a brief discussion of lawyers and tattoos, *see* Jennifer W. Reynolds, *The Lawyer with the ADR Tattoo*, CARDOZO JOURNAL OF CONFLICT RESOLUTION, Winter 2013 ("Tattoos have historic associations with 'sailors, criminals, ..., and circus entertainers,' none of which are generally in keeping with what most believe a lawyer ought to look like.").

5. *Id.* ("Although more than 45 million Americans today have a tattoo, and although 'creative' professions such as marketing and graphic design have readily adopted tattoo culture, more conservative industries such as law and finance still do not welcome visible tattoos in the workplace.... As one anonymous online poster put it, '[I]f I walked into a lawyer's office and noticed a lawyer had a tattoo[,] I would walk straight out again.' ").

included them again here so that you will have a complete list to work with. Although undergarments, hosiery, and socks are not included in the following lists, please remember that they, too, are a very important part of your professional wardrobe.

Women

Belts	Black-Tie Attire
Blazers	Blouses
Boots	*Coats*
Cocktail Dress	Day Dresses
Handbag	Keychain
Scarves	*Shoes*
Skirts	Slacks
Suits	Sweaters
T-Shirts	Wallet
Watch	

Men

Belts	Black-Tie Attire
Blazers	*Coats*
Keychain	Neckties
Shirts	*Shoes*
Slacks	*Suits*
Sweaters	T-Shirts
Wallet	*Watch*
Winter Scarf	

Keeping Your Professional Wardrobe Organized

If you've ever seen the film *Mommie Dearest*, you probably remember the scene depicting Joan Crawford's clear disdain for the use of wire hangers. While her reaction is more than a little extreme, Ms. Crawford was right about not using wire hangers because they can harm the line of your clothing by causing the hangers to bend from the weight. Dry cleaners presumably use wire hangers because they're cheap and expendable—and not intended for permanent use. If at all possible, invest in wooden hangers. You can also save and use the plastic hangers that come with clothing you are purchasing for your professional wardrobe. They are plentiful and free, and they are much easier on your clothing than wire hangers.

For clothing that may be folded, such as sweaters, t-shirts, and casual pants, each organizational type will have different challenges. Stackers will dutifully fold and store items in neat stacks, but they will need to ensure that the piles do not develop into small mountains that can topple over into large messes that must be re-folded. Spreaders will hang clothing that they do not regularly wear, but they can create messes by taking things off of hangers and laying them around as they make decisions, leaving a mess to contend with afterward. Free Spirits and Packrats need to designate places in which to store their clothing, and they need to work hard to hang their clothing neatly.

Chapter Checklist

✓ Whether you're meeting with clients or sequestered in your office working on a brief, it's crucial that you look the part of an attorney who is polished, professional, and in control.

• Look through your closet to determine what is working for and against you as you work to sharpen your professional appearance.

• Check with your firm or company to see whether there is a dress code policy, and also verify whether there are policies to adhere to when visiting clients in their places of business.

• Develop a clear understanding of "business casual" attire.

• Consider purchasing items in the "Shopping List" and "Wardrobe Staples" sections.

• Avoid the use of wire hangers in an effort to preserve your clothing.

• Conceal tattoos and body piercings, particularly in conservative work environments.

• Remain mindful of the challenges in clothing maintenance based on your organizational type.

Old habits cannot be thrown out the upstairs window. They have to be coaxed downstairs one step at a time.

Mark Twain (Samuel Clemens)

CHAPTER 12

JUST THE BEGINNING

Throughout this book, we have addressed many elements of organization, including determining how you live among your things, methods for organizing these items, and the challenges you may face in keeping them that way. Although you've reached the end of the book, this is only the beginning.

Like other terms we have explored, "organization" is both a noun and a verb. It is a process that requires constant exploration, tweaking, and decision making. It takes a lot of time and thought on the front end, but this work will pay great dividends each time you set foot into your home and office workspaces.

The legal profession is busy and demanding, and it can be very easy to become overwhelmed with all of the competing projects and responsibilities. If and when that happens, be easy on yourself, but don't give up on this organizational process. No matter how busy or tired you become, spending five minutes tidying up your home and office workspaces before leaving them can make all the difference in the sense of control you feel about work, in general.

We have covered a lot of ground in the preceding chapters, so you may need to revisit various sections from time to time as your needs and interests change and evolve. You may also want to share this book with your assistant, loved ones, or anyone else you may work or partner with on projects on a regular basis so that they can gain a better understanding of this process and the great strides you are making to become and remain more organized. You might also ask them to take the Organization Questionnaire to see how your styles mesh (and also possibly clash) for an increased understanding of mutual needs. For example, Packrats may gain a clearer appreciation for the frustrations that may be felt by a spouse who is a Stacker, and vice versa. A better understanding in this regard can also enable different types to help each other to stay motivated and stick with the organizational process.

During the Introduction, we set out to explore and resolve three issues: (1) What does it mean to be organized? (2) Why does it matter? (3) How are lawyers different? Through your reading and self-exploration, I hope I have helped to clarify and confirm the following answers. First, organization has visual and conceptual elements, and it is not enough to simply "know where everything is." There are many people who use this notion as an excuse for not doing what it takes to develop a system that looks as great as it supposedly works. The perceptions of clients and colleagues matter. It is not enough to *be* organized. You must also *appear to be* organized to receive the most benefits from this process. Second, good organization matters because it helps you get your work done more efficiently in a space that makes you feel more at peace and in control, which directly impacts your performance, client satisfaction, and reputation as a legal professional.

Finally, lawyers are different in several ways. They tend to wrestle with challenges privately.[1] As the "go to" people for the problems others face, many tend to keep their own dilemmas to themselves because they are accustomed to having the answers for others. This process of feeling required to have all the answers begins in law school. We all remember the terrible shame that resulted from being called on in class when we were unprepared and the huge sense of embarrassment we felt when we did not know the answer to the question posed. We spent hours reading and preparing for classes so that we would not be caught unaware again. Although a lack of organization is not the same as a case we might study, it is an example of a problem that requires exploration and answers. For some of us, it may perhaps cause even greater frustration because we assume it should be easier to master this than the law because we incorrectly think it only involves cleaning. As you now know, it's not that simple.

---

1. *See* Daicoff, *supra* Chapter 1, n.1.

Like the law, organization is a topic with many layers and nuances, and it impacts us all a little differently. We know what it looks like, but it takes time, honesty, and effort to achieve. Similarly, lawyers know how to define the law and what an effective law entails, but they also realize that these same laws took a lot of time and effort to get on the books, and they will continue to be reevaluated and fine tuned over time. Like good organizational skills, the creation and practice of law are a process. When combined, law and organization together make better lawyers, happier clients, and result in fewer complaints of malpractice or other violations of the Rules of Professional Conduct.

The legal profession can only benefit from an increased effort from attorneys in all practice areas to become and remain organized. An increased awareness of good organizational skills geared toward the needs of lawyers and the resulting benefits from being organized will have long-lasting and positive results for lawyers and everyone around them. It may also contribute to a decrease in stress in the profession and feelings of being overwhelmed with projects that are out of control.

If you had the wherewithal to get through law school, then you have the stamina and fortitude it will take to become organized. It all starts with picking up one sheet of paper, clearing out a small desk drawer, or simply ceasing to wear an article of clothing that no longer flatters you. But it must be something you want to do in order to continue to stick with it, and there are many potential results to keep you motivated.

A well-organized space provides a sense of control and order, and there's nothing like coming into your offices at home and work and having a good idea of the whereabouts of everything you need so that all you have to do is focus on the job at hand. It feels good when colleagues and clients come into your office and seem impressed by how nice it looks. It feels great when you don't have to shove items aside to offer someone a seat in your office. These are the feelings that will keep you working to ensure your space remains organized.

If you have followed the steps outlined in this book, you have already made great progress in your goal of becoming an organized lawyer. You know your organizational type and how that impacts your tendencies and choices. You're familiar with office layouts and desk arrangements both at home and at work. You have sorted through paper and electronic files and selected a planner or an electronic organizer. You have created a portable office for times when you must work in alternative environments. You've also become much more aware of legal event planning and ways to maximize these events in an organized way and to your benefit. You are also creating an organized professional wardrobe so that you "look the part" to colleagues and clients.

Invariably, there will be times when you become a little lax or fall off the organizational wagon, but that does not mean you are destined for a messy workspace for life. Keep at it. Remember, as a lawyer, you have what it takes to do this.

As I mentioned the Introduction, this book is designed to be used as you see fit, and small efforts mean a lot. Once your space is organized, it should take minimal time to keep it that way. Typically, if you can commit five minutes at the end of the day and less than an hour at the end of the week to maintaining your home and work offices, you can keep them organized.

Your success is of particular interest to me, and I would be delighted to hear how this book has helped you. Please send comments to organizedlawyer@gmail.com, or visit www.theorganized lawyer.com.

As a lawyer, you are smart, focused, and driven. As an organized lawyer, you will not only enhance your own practice, but you will also make a positive impact on the future of the legal profession. It is up to you, and it starts now. So, to repeat the question I initially posed at the end of the Introduction, are you ready to begin?

Index